Dictionary *of* Beer *and* Brewing

The Association of Brewers'

Dictionary

of

Beer

and

Brewing

The Most Complete Collection
of Brewing Terms Written in English

Compiled by Carl Forget

WITHDRAWN

Brewers Publications
Boulder, Colorado

Association of Brewers'
Dictionary of Beer and Brewing
by Carl Forget

Copyright © 1988 by Carl Forget
ISBN 0-937381-10-1
Printed in the United States of America
10 9 8 7 6 5 4 3

Published by Brewers Publications,
a division of the Association of Brewers Inc.,
PO Box 1679, Boulder, Colorado 80306-1679 USA
(303) 447-0816 • FAX: (303) 447-2825

Cover design by Susie Marcus
Cover photograph by Michael Lichter

Acknowledgments

Special thanks to Lois Canaday for stylistic editing, and to George Fix and Charlie Papazian for technical review and editing.

Contents

Introduction

Every now and then, we have the opportunity to publish a book that makes an outstanding contribution to both amateur brewing and the international professional brewing industry. *The Association of Brewers' Dictionary of Beer and Brewing* is such a book.

With its treasure of 1,929 definitions, the *Dictionary* is the first and most complete collection of brewing terms written in the English language.

The *Dictionary's* value to brewers is obvious. Now we have at our fingertips the essential definitions of the terms we use in beer recipes and brewing processes.

The Dictionary also has another use — sheer entertainment. If you're like me, you'll be delighted with reading the definitions of arcane and ancient brewing terms such as Purl, Radlermass, coirm, prima melior, Mertzbier, hippocras. In these definitions resides the evolution of the brewing process and products throughout various centuries and cultures.

On another level, however, the Dictionary holds enormous value for brewers collectively. For the first time, English-speaking brewers have easy access to a point of reference — a common brewing language never before available to us. Compiled by professional lexiconist Carl Forgét, the Dictionary will be a brewers tool for years to come. It gives me great pride, as publisher, to be able to offer a work of this quality and usefulness.

Charlie Papazian, Publisher

a-acid. Abbreviation form of alpha acid.

A.A.U. Abbreviation for alpha acid unit.

abbey beer. Any top- or bottom-fermented beer produced by a commercial brewery under license from a monastery, located near an abbey or that has retained the original name and brewing style of a particular abbey. In Belgium, according to a law passed in Gand on February 28, 1962, beers brewed in Trappist monasteries or by commercial breweries under license may be labeled *Trappiste* while those brewed by commercial brewers in the style and manner of trappist beers must be labeled *bière d'abbaye* or *abdijbieren* (abbey beer). There are presently five Trappist abbeys brewing beer in Belgium and one across the Dutch border. In Germany and Austria, beers labeled *Klosterbräu* or *Stiftsbräu* are not distinctive in style nor are they brewed, for the most part, in abbeys. **Syn**: monastery beer. **See also**: Trappist beer.

abdijbieren. See: abbey beer.

absolute alcohol. 1. Pure, water-free ethyl alcohol. Specific gravity: 0.79359; boiling point: 78.4°C (173.12°F). The American standard is 200 proof while the British standard is 175.1 proof. **Syn**: anhydrous alcohol. **2.** The total amount of alcohol contained in a beverage.

aca. A type of maize beer brewed in Peru since at least 200 BC. It was consumed by the common people and the Sapa-Inca; it also was offered to the Gods and poured over the graves of the deceased mojicas. The aca of the Sapa-Inca could only be prepared by the Sun Virgins of the palace in Cuzco. **See also**: chicha.

acerbic. Descriptive of a bitter, somewhat astringent taste in beer, less pronounced than acidic.

acetaldehyde. A volatile compound derived from the degradation of sugars during fermentation through decarboxylation of pyruvic acid. **Syn:** ethylaldehyde. **See also:** aldehyde; carbonyls.

acetic. Imparting a smell of acetic acid or ethyl acetate.

acetic acid. Formula: CH_3COOH. A weak, monocarboxylic acid found in vinegar. It is the first member of the fatty acid series and also belongs to the larger group of carboxylic acids. This acid is a natural by-product of yeast metabolism, being formed with the Krebs cycle during aerobic respiration. In beermaking, it forms through oxidation of alcohols during the fermentation process giving the beer a vinegar taste and smell.

Acetobacter. A microorganism, a genus of aerobic bacteria (*Bacteriaceae* family), that turns ethyl alcohol to acetic acid during fermentation.

acid. 1. Any compound that yields hydrogen ions (H^+) in solution or a chemical that reacts with alkalis to form salts. 2. Is said of a solution having a pH lower than 7.0. **See also:** pH. 3. Descriptive of a beer exhibiting a sour acidic smell or flavor.

acidic. Descriptive of a beer having a biting, sour or pungent aroma and flavor reminiscent of vinegar or acetic acid. **Syn:** sour.

acidification. The process of lowering the pH of a solution until it falls below 7.0.

acidity. 1. The state of being acid or the extent to which a solution is acid. **See also:** pH. 2. In beer tasting, the degree of sharpness to the taste.

acid malt. A type of malt prepared by various methods and used, mainly, at a rate 10% or less to lower the pH in the mash tun. One method consists of spraying the growing malt with 10% lactic acid followed by steeping in a solution of lactic acid prior to kilning.

acrospire. The shoot contained within the embryo of the barley grain and which, during germination, is allowed to grow up to two-thirds or three-fourths the length of the corn kernel beneath the husk before kilning. **Syn:** plumule.

activator. A substance that increases the effectiveness or activity of an enzyme.

Adam's ale. A misnomer for water.

Adam's wine. A misnomer for water.

additive. Any chemical, natural or synthetic, deliberately added to beer in the course of production, packaging or storing for a specific reason. Most legislations exclude food ingredients (nutritive materials) such as salt, sugar, vitamins, minerals, amino acids, spices, seasonings, flavorings, food enhancers and others which fall into another category covered by food regulations. **Syn:** food additive.

adjunct. Any substitute *unmalted* cereal grain or fermentable ingredient added to the mash for the purpose of reducing costs by producing more, usually cheaper, fermentable sugars and/or to produce paler, lighter-bodied and less malty beers or, as is the case of wheat, to produce special beers or to correct the composition of the extract. Oats, wheat, corn, tapioca flour, flaked rice and maize, inverted sugar and glucose are used for this purpose. The external part of the maize is particularly rich in starch. Most cereal adjuncts saccharify very slowly in the mash and must first be gelatinized by boiling before they can be attacked by amylases. To avoid pre-boiling, maize and a few other cereals are added in the form of flakes. In Belgium the amount of unmalted cereals added to the grist varies between 10 to 20% while French and American beers contain 30 to 40% adjuncts. In Germany the use of adjuncts is prohibited by law. **Syn**: malt adjunct; cereal adjunct.

Adriaan Brouwer Bierfesten. An annual beer festival held June 25-27 in Oudenaarde, Belgium, to commemorate the famous painter born in that city in 1605.

adsorption. The surface retention of solid, liquid or gas molecules by another surface without any chemical reaction with the adsorption material. Adsorption substances are used for fining and filtration. They include activated charcoal, silica gel, albumin, bentonite, kieselguhr and similar substances.

aerating. The action of providing aeration.

aeration. 1. The action of impregnating with or exposing to air at various stages of the brewing process. Aerating the cooled wort, for example, favors the growth and multiplication of yeast cells during aerobic (primary) fermentation. **2.** An operation introducing air into a mass of barley grains at a rate of flow adequate to achieve and maintain levels of temperature and humidity required for satisfactory storage.

aerobic. Occurring in the presence of air (or oxygen), such as in primary fermentation when yeast cells require oxygen to grow and multiply. **See also:** aerobic fermentation; anaerobic.

aerobic fermentation. Any fermentation process requiring the presence of air (i.e., oxygen) such as primary fermentation.

aerobiosis. Life existing in the presence of air and oxygen. **See also:** anaerobiosis.

aftertaste. The taste, odor and tactile sensations that linger after the beer has been swallowed.

aftersmell. An odor sensation that lingers after swallowing the beer, possibly caused by remaining volatiles.

agar(-agar). A colloidal gel obtained from the dried, putrefied stems of a red seaweed (*Gelidium algae, Graciloria*) growing in Japanese waters and used for fining purposes or as a culture medium for bacteria and yeasts. **Syn:** Madagascar gum; vegetable gelatine.

aged flavor. Synonym for off-flavor.

aging. Synonym for maturation.

airing. The action of ventilating the barley between steeps. **Syn:** ventilation.

airlock. Synonym for fermentation lock.

air rest. An interruption in the steeping process to allow oxygen to get through and stimulate growth and a uniform germination. This technique, now regarded as traditional, was first developed in the early 1960s to overcome dormancy in water-sensitive types of barley. **See also:** airing; steeping.

airspace. Synonym for ullage.

airtight. So constructed or sealed as to prevent the inlet and outlet of air.

albumen. 1. Orthographic variant for albumin. 2. The starchy content of the barley grain.

albumin. A name for a certain group of water-soluble proteins which coagulate when heated. Albumins are hydrolized to peptides and amino acids by proteolytic enzymes.

alcohol. A synonym for ethyl alcohol or ethanol. Etym: From the Arabic *al kohl* meaning like kohl (an eye cosmetic paint) because the method of distillation by vaporizing native brew was similar to that for producing kohl.

alcohol beverage. Synonym for alcoholic beverage.

alcohol by volume. A measurement of the alcohol content of a solution in terms of the percentage volume of alcohol per volume of beer. To approximately calculate (margin of error ±15%) the volumetric alcohol content, subtract the terminal gravity from the original gravity and divide the result by 7.5. Abbrev: v/v. **See** conversion table at the end of the book.
  Formula: % v/v = (OG - TG)/ 7.5.
  Example: 50 - 12 = 38 / 7.5 = 5% v/v.

alcohol by weight. A measurement of the alcohol content of a solution in terms of the percentage weight of alcohol per volume of beer. Example: 3.2% alcohol by weight = 3.2 grams of alcohol per 100 centiliters of beer. The percent of alcohol by weight figure is approximately 20% lower than the "by volume" figure because alcohol weighs less than its equivalent volume of water. Abbrev: w/v. **See** conversion table at the end of the book.

alcohol content. The amount of ethyl alcohol contained in a beverage. In beer, it is related to the specific gravity of the wort prior to fermentation (called original gravity), which usually varies from 1.030 to 1.060 but may reach 1.100. Beer fermentation is self-limiting because beyond 12% to 16% alcohol by volume, yeast cells suffocate in the alcohol and die. Alcohol tolerance depends on yeast strain. **Syn:** alcoholic strength.

alcoholic beverage. Any potable beverage containing ethyl alcohol produced by fermentation of sugars such as beer, wine, mead, cider and others or by distillation of these products. Fermented beverages may contain up to 16% alcohol by volume at which point the yeast is killed. **Syn:** alcohol beverage; beverage alcohol.

alcoholic strength. The alcoholic strength of beers is measured, in America and Germany, in percent alcohol by weight, while Canada and the United Kingdom refer to its volumetric content. In the United Kingdom the specific gravity (or density) method is used. This measurement system attributes the number 1000 to water and the density of beers is measured in comparison to that standard. An approximate formula for converting beer densities to alcohol by weight consists in dividing the last two figures of the density by 13 (Ex: s.g. 1052 = 52 / 13 = 4.0% w/v). Other systems such as degrees Plato (°P), derived from the Balling system, measure the concentration of solids in unfermented worts. An approximate formula for converting degrees Plato to percent alcohol by weight is obtained by dividing the former by 3 (12°P / 3 = 4% w/v). **See also:** Belgian degrees; Régie.

alcoholimeter. Orthographic variant for alcoholometer.

alcoholmeter. Orthographic variant for alcoholometer.

alcoholometer. An instrument, such as a densimeter or hydrometer, for measuring the amount of ethyl alcohol in a solution. It consists of a graduated stem expressing the percentage of alcohol by weight or by volume resting on a spindle-shaped float. Also spelled: alcohometer; alcoholimeter; alcoholmeter.

alcoholometry. The quantitative determination of ethyl alcohol in aqueous solutions, usually by measuring the specific gravity of the solution at a standard temperature with an alcoholometer.

alcohols. See: higher alcohols.

alcohometer. Orthographic variant for alcoholometer.

aldehyde. Any of a large class of organic compounds derived from alcohols through dehydrogenation (oxidation) and containing the grouping (or radical) -CHO. When aldehydes are oxidized further, acids are produced. Some aldehydes contribute to the bouquet of beer. Etym: From ALcohol and DEHYDrogenation.

aldehyde dehydrogenase. An enzyme that catalyzes the oxidative conversion of an aldehyde to its corresponding acid in the metabolism of ethanol.

ale. 1. Historically, a nonhopped malt beverage (also called *spiced ale*) as opposed to hopped beer. 2. A generic name for beers produced by top fermentation, usually by infusion mashing, as opposed to lagers produced by bottom fermentation, usually by decoction mashing. Ales tend to have higher alcoholic contents, more robust flavor and deeper hues than lagers. It is the style predominant in the British Isles. Ales constitute a category including alt, barley wine, bitter, brown beer, Kölsch, mild ale, pale ale, porter, stout, Trappist beer and others. **3.** In America, some state legislations prohibit the use of the name lager or beer for malt beverages containing more than 5.0% alcohol by weight and such beverages are often labeled as ales although they are bottom-fermented (lager) beers. Etym: Derived from the Norse *oel* (Danish and Swedish *öl* ; Finnish *olut*), a nonhopped malt beverage. The Vikings called their barley beer *aul* . The Anglo-Saxon word for ale was *ealu*. **Syn**: top-fermented beer. **See also**: top fermentation; top-fermenting yeast; lager.

ale barrel. In England, a barrel containing 32 imperial gallons (146.47 liters) not to be confused with a beer barrel that contains 36 imperial gallons (163.65 liters).

aleberry. An old-fashioned drink popular in England in the 1600s consisting of oatmeal, ale, lemon juice, nutmeg and sugar served hot with sops of toast. It also was known as alebrue and alemeat.

ale-bowl. An early drinking vessel for ale.

ale-brewer. One who brews ales. In 15th century England, when hops were beginning to be accepted for beermaking, there was a clear distinction between ale-brewers, who brewed unhopped spiced ales, and beer-brewers who brewed *hopping* beers. Beer-brewers were persecuted at every opportunity but luckily for them their brew was considered by many as superior to ale. In 1436, the King issued a wit to the sheriffs of London ordering them to protect the beer-brewers. **Syn**: ale-maker.

ale-bush. Synonym for ale garland.

ale-conner. In old England, an official appointed by the authorities of the city or borough to inspect and judge newly brewed ale to be sold by the ale-makers. In the 14th century the ale-conner wore leather breeches and tested the ale by pouring it on a bench and sitting in the puddle for half an hour. If upon rising the breeches stuck to the bench the ale was sugary and imperfect; otherwise, it was fit for consumption. Shakespeare's father was an ale-conner in Stratford-on-Avon in 1557. Also spelled: aleconner.

alecost. An obsolete name for costmary (*Tanacetum balsamica, Balsamita vulgaris* or *Chrysanthemum balsamita*) once used to flavor ales in England.

ale draper. An ale-house keeper.

Ale Flip. A cocktail consisting of one or half a pint of ale mixed, in a shaker, with crushed ice and one egg.

alegar. An obsolete word for spoiled, sour ale.

ale garland. An ivy-bush or garland of evergreens placed at the top of a pole called ale-stake outside an ale-house. **Syn**: ale-bush.

ale-gill. A type of ale once flavored with ground ivy.

ale glass. A long and narrow stemmed glass for serving old ale.

alehoof. An early name given to ground ivy used to flavor ales.

ale-house. A public house where beer is sold. In early England, the term brewery referred to both the brew-house and the room in which the ale was sold, which later became known as an ale-house. Licenses to operate ale-houses have been issued as early as the 14th century. In 1305 one William Saleman was fined two shillings for operating a brewery on Cornwill without a license. Later such licenses were issued by the Justice of the Peace. Also spelled: alehouse. **Rare syn**: bush-house. **See also**: Brewster Sessions.

ale jug. Synonym for beer jug.

ale knight. An obsolete term referring to a person who frequents ale-houses and whose knighthood comes from conquering ale glasses.

ale-maker. Synonym for ale-brewer.

Ale Nog. A cocktail. One recipe suggests 1 liter of ale, 4 coffeespoons of milk, 100 grams of sugar, 8 egg yolks and nutmeg. The egg yolks and sugar are mixed and beaten; the ale is added slowly while still beating and finally the nutmeg for flavor.

ale passion. A slang term for a headache caused by ale drinking.

ale-pole. Synonym for ale-stake.

ale posset. See: posset.

ale-post. Synonym for ale-stake.

ale-stake. In old England, a branch, stick or pole placed outside a house to indicate that ale had been freshly brewed there. The practice dates back to Saxon times when wayside taverns or ale-houses erected on Roman roads were identified by means of a long pole. If wine was sold along with mead and ale an ivy-bush was hung atop the pole. In the 14th century the same bush or ivy-plant was a sign for the ale-conner and customers that a fresh brew was ready. In London, in 1375, a city ordinance prescribed that such poles should not extend more than seven feet in length. **Syn also:** ale-pole; ale-post.

aleurone. The protein reserve in the form of granules or grains contained within the aleurone layer.

aleurone layer. The single, outer layer of large cells containing the starchy endosperm. It is situated just below the surface of the grain and constitutes 2 to 3% of its weight. **Syn:** proteinaceous layer.

ale warmer. A conical vessel with a handle made of thinned brass or copper and formerly used to warm ale over a fire in a grate. **Syn:** ass's ear.

ale wife. In medieval England, a woman who brewed ale, one who kept a tavern or a combination of both. The term is usually synonymous with brewster and breweress, although it sometimes refers to women who simply sold ale on the premises where it was made as opposed to a hukster. From 1300 onward, ale-wives found guilty of over-charging or pitching a mug were severely punished, apparently more so than male brewers. Punishment could be a fine or the ducking-stool (or cucking stool). The practice of ducking persisted well into the 18th century. Also spelled: alewife. **Syn**: brewster; breweress. **See also**: hukster.

ale yard. Synonym for yard-of-ale. Also spelled: aleyard.

ale yeast. Synonym for top fermenting yeast.

algin. An insoluble colloidal substance obtained from a brown marine algae (*Phaophyceae*) and sometimes used for clarifying beer. **Syn**: alginic acid.

alginic acid. Synonym for algin.

algarroba beer. A type of beer brewed in Central and South America from the sweet ripe beans of the carob, mesquite or other leguminous trees, especially those of the Prosopis species. It is the sacred drink of the Chaco tribes and is forbidden to women. Also spelled: algorobo beer.

alixone. An old French name for a type of beer made in the Middle Ages.

alkali. Any compound that yields hydroxyl (OH) ions in a solution or a chemical that reacts with acids to form salts.

alkaline. 1. Is said of a solution having a pH greater than 7.0. **See also**: pH. **2.** Describes a beer that has retained traces of an alkali from the brewing liquor.

alkalinity. The extent to which a solution is alkaline.

all-extract beer. A beer made entirely from malt extract as opposed to one made from barley, or from malt extract and barley.

all-grain beer. A beer made entirely from malt as opposed to one made from malt extract, or from malt extract and malted barley.

all-malt beer. A beer made entirely from barley malt without the addition of adjuncts or sugars.

Alost. A variety of hops grown in Flanders, Belgium.

alpha acid. One of the two resins in hops. It consists of a mixture of three closely related chemical compounds, humulone, cohumulone and adhumulone and forms 2 to 14% of the total weight of hop cones and approximately 45% of their soft resins. Although the relative proportion of adhumulone is fairly constant at 15%, the proportion of humulone and cohumulone vary from one hop variety to another. For example, the cohumulone content of Northern Brewer is close to 40% while that of Fuggles is about 30%. Alpha acids have a low wort solubility, and about 90% of beer bitterness is caused by compounds that form during boiling, the most important of which are iso-alpha-acids (isohumu-lones), which account for 60% of beer bitterness. The conversion of alpha-acids to iso-alpha-acids takes from one to one and a half hours; however, this may vary because the solubility of alpha acids decreases with increasing wort gravity. In commercial brewing, isohumulones are sometimes added in the form of isomerized extracts, usually after fermentation. Upon aging, alpha acids oxidize and lose approximately 30% of their bittering power after one year and about 40% after two years. Abbrev: a-acid. **Syn**: humulon(e); alpha resin. **See also**: beta acid; soft resins.

alpha acid unit. A measurement of the potential bitterness of hops expressed in terms of their percentage alpha acid content. Low = 2 to 4%, medium = 5 to 7%, high = 8 to 12%. Abbrev: A.A.U. **See also**: bitterness units; bittering units; homebrewers bittering units; hop bitterness coefficient; hop bitterness units.

alpha-amylase. A diastatic enzyme produced by malting barley, also known as liquefying enzyme because it converts soluble malt starch into complex car-bohydrates called dextrins during mashing. Alpha-amylases work best at high pH (5.6 to 5.8) and at high temperature (65.6°C, 150°F). They can withstand temperatures in excess of 73°C (163°F) but are destroyed at 80°C (176°F). **Syn**: liquefying enzyme; dextrinogenic amylase. **See also**: amylase; beta-amylase.

alpha resin. Synonym for alpha acid.

Alt. Synonym for Altbier.

Altbier. A traditional style of beer brewed mainly in Düsseldorf but also in Münster, Korschenbroich, Krefeld, Issum and a few other cities of Northern Rhineland and Westphalia. The German word *alt* means old or ancient and refers to the fact that these beers are brewed by the traditional method of top fermentation predating the relatively new method of bottom fermentation introduced in the mid-18th century and now predominant throughout Ger-many. Alt beers have a deep, luminous, copper color. They are brewed from dark malts, are well hopped and display a slightly fruity, bittersweet flavor. Their alcohol content varies from 3.5 to 4.0% by weight (4.4 to 5.0% v/v) and are brewed from an original gravity of about 12.5° Balling. Those from Düsseldorf have Echte Düsseldorfer Altbier written on the label. **Syn**: Düsseldorfer Alt(bier); Alt.

amasaké. In Japan, a sweet, non-alcoholic, saké-like beverage flavored with ginger. The term means "sweet saké." Also spelled: amazaké.

amateur brewer. Synonym for homebrewer.

amazaké. Orthographic variant for amasaké.

amber beer. A general name for any top- or bottom-fermented beer displaying an amber color, halfway betwen pale and dark. Copper-colored or coppery are sometimes synonymous but these words suggest a more reddish hue.

amber malt. Malt prepared from well-modified malt containing 3 to 4% moisture that is dried rapidly at high temperature, usually around 93.3°C (200°F), for 15 to 20 minutes and then gradually to 138 to 149°C (280 to 300°F) for a long period during which time the embryo and some enzymes are killed, thus imparting a slightly burnt or "biscuit" flavor to beer.

amines. Volatiles found in beer, most of which are derived from ammonia originating from malt and hops through replacement of one or more hydrogen atoms by organic radicals. Amines form during the germination process. It has been suggested that they are responsible for the characteristic aroma of germinated barley. The concentration of volatile amines is greater in hops than in malt, and Fuggles has the highest concentration followed by Alsace, Backa, and Hallertauer.

amino acid. Any of the organic acids whose molecules contain one or more acidic carboxyl groups (COOH) and one or more amino groups (NH_2) and that polymerize to form peptides and proteins. Proteins are macromolecules composed of combinations of large numbers of twenty different natural amino acids. During the beermaking process, amino acids are formed by the enzymatic degradation of such proteins. During kilning, amino acids combine with simple sugars to form colored compounds called melanoidins. Of the 80 amino acids found in nature, eight are considered to be essential in the diet (essential amino acids are identified by an asterisk in the table below), another 12 are considered nonessential. The critical issue associated with amino acids is their rate of uptake by yeast and the role they play in metabolism. Some amino acids are not essential because yeast can produce their carbon skeletons during metabolism. Others are essential in the sense that they can come only from malt. All amino acids are used by yeast, as nutrients, at different parts of the fermentation.

Amino Acids	Abbrev.	Molecular Weight	Solubility
alanine	Ala	89.09	Very soluble
arginine	Arg	174.14	Very soluble
aspartic acid	Asp	133.07	Slightly soluble
cystine	Cys	240.30	Almost insoluble
glutamic acid	Glu	147.08	Slightly soluble
glycine	Gly	76.07	Very soluble
histidine	His	155.09	Soluble
hydroxylysine	Hyl	162.19	Very soluble
hydroxyproline	Hyp	131.08	Very soluble
isoleucine*	Ile	131.11	Slightly soluble
leucine*	Leu	131.11	Slightly soluble
lysine*	Lys	146.19	Very soluble

*essential amino acids

Amino Acids	Abbrev.	Molecular Weight	Solubility
methionine*	Met	149.15	Soluble
phenylalanine*	Phe	165.19	Slightly soluble
proline	Pro	115.08	Very soluble
threonine*	Thr	119.08	Very soluble
tryptophane*	Trp	204.11	Very slightly soluble
tyrosine	Tyr	181.19	Almost insoluble
valine*	Val	117.09	Soluble

* essential amino acids

amyl acetate. Formula: $CH_3COOC_5H_{11}$. An amylic ester derived from acetic acid and responsible for the "fruity" or "banana" odor in beer. **Syn**: banana oil; banana ester. **See also**: butyl acetate.

amylase. A generic name for alpha- and beta-amylase, enzymes that hydrolize starch into maltose. Alpha-amylase converts insoluble and soluble starch into dextrins and maltotriose, and then beta-amylase hydrolizes the dextrins into glucose, maltose, maltotriose and limit dextrins. The complete degradation of starch requires both alpha- and beta-amylase. Amylases are also present in saliva, which accounts for the practice of mastication in primitive times to induce fermentation in beery substances. **See also**: alpha-amylase; beta-amylase, diastase.

amylodextrin. A very complex dextrin produced by the amylolytic hydrolysis of starch.

amyloglucosidase. A type of amylase available commercially, a typical fungal enzyme with temperature optima between 40 and 50°C (104 to 122°F). When added to fermenting wort it splits dextrins into fermentable sugars, thus producing a highly alcoholic and low caloric (diatetic) beer devoid of dextrins. **Syn**: glucoamylase.

amylolysis. The enzymatic hydrolysis of starch into glucose, maltose and dextrins.

amylolytic. Characteristic applied to enzymes that convert starch to soluble substances. **Syn**: diastatic.

amylolytic enzyme. An enzyme that converts starch into soluble substances, mainly sugars. **See also**: proteolytic enzyme.

amylopectin. The branched-chain fraction of starch that is relatively insoluble in water. Barley contains about 73% amylopectin, wheat 75%, rice 83%, and maize 78%. The other fraction is amylose.

amylose. The straight-chain fraction of starch that is relatively soluble. Barley contains about 27% amylose, wheat 25%, rice 17%, and maize 22%. The other fraction is amylopectin.

anaerobic. Occurring in the absence of air (or oxygen) as in secondary fermentation.

anaerobic fermentation. A generic name for any fermentation process that takes place without the presence of air, i.e., does not require dissolved oxygen. In beermaking, the secondary fermentation is of this type.

anaerobiosis. Life existing in the absence of air or oxygen. **See also:** aerobiosis.

anhydrous alcohol. Synonym for absolute alcohol.

anion. A negatively-charged ion.

antelmann. An instrument for measuring the length of the acrospire of germinating barley. The maltster uses the growth of the acrospire as a rough guide to estimate the progress of the germination process, which is usually stopped by kilning before the acrospire grows beyond the end of the grain.

antifreeze. A substance added to an aqueous solution to lower its freezing point. In brewing, calcium chloride and glycol are sometimes added to beer for this purpose.

antioxidant. A reducing agent added in small amounts to bottled beer to delay or prevent oxidation. Antioxidants are commonly used to retard the oxidative rancidity of fats. I-ascorbic acid (vitamin C) and the sulfites (sulfur dioxide, potassium metabisulfite, bisulfite) are used for this purpose. Also spelled: anti-oxidant.

antiseptic. A substance used to destroy or prevent growth of infectious microorganisms or bacteria.

Apache beer. See: tiswin.

apparent attenuation. The attenuation of beer containing alcohol but no carbon dioxide. It is apparent because it does not represent the extract lost during fermentation, since the drop in gravity caused by the transformation of sugars is added to that of alcohol, which is lighter than water (0.79 at 15°C). Apparent attenuation can be converted to real attenuation by multiplying it by 0.819. Since it is easier to measure than real attenuation, it is the method commonly used by brewers, and the term attenuation without qualification invariably means apparent attenuation.

Formula: $A = (B - b)/B \times 100$

A = apparent attenuation in %
B = original gravity in °B (or Plato)
b = gravity of beer devoid of CO_2

appealing. Descriptive of a pleasant, easy-drinking beer, containing no off-flavors or odors.

appetizing. Describes a beer suitable for serving as an apéritif because it whets the appetite.

aqueous. Consisting of or comprising water; dissolved in water.

aroma. The pleasant fragrance of beer that originates from the natural odors of its ingredients — barley, malt and hops. **See also:** bouquet.

aroma hops. Synonym for finishing hops.

aromatic hops. Synonym for finishing hops.

artificial saturation. Carbon dioxide gas dissolved into beer by pressure, usually to compensate for a lack of it at the end of secondary fermentation.

asbestos filter. A type of filter consisting of layers of asbestos fiber sheets through which beer is pumped.

ascorbic acid. Formula: $C_6H_8O_6$. A water-soluble vitamin occurring naturally in many plants, especially citrus fruits, or made synthetically from glucose. It has mild reducing properties and is added to finished beer to prevent or delay oxidation and partly to clear the beer of dissolved oxygen. **Syn:** l-ascorbic acid; vitamin C; L-xyloascorbic acid.

ash. The residue left behind after all the organic matter of a substance has been incinerated. It consists of mineral matter and serves as a measure of the inorganic salts that were in the original substance.

ass's ear. Synonym for ale warmer.

astringent. In beer, a harsh, mouth-puckering sensation. **Syn:** harsh; tannic; austere.

astringency. A characteristic of beer taste mostly caused by tannins, oxidized tannins (phenols) and various aldehydes (in stale beer) that cause the mouth to pucker.

attemperating coil. A type of heat exchanger consisting of a series of spiral-coiled pipes inserted, when needed, into vats to heat or cool the solution within. **Syn:** attemperator.

attemperator. **1.** A small, ice-filled container immersed in bottom fermenting beer to maintain a constant temperature of 6-7°C (43-45°F). It was replaced in the 1970s by attemperating coils. **Syn:** swimmer. **2.** Synonym for attemperating coil.

attenuation. The percentage reduction in the wort's specific gravity caused by the transformation of contained sugars into alcohol and carbon dioxide gas through fermentation. The fermentable sugars in the wort (which have a higher specific gravity than water) are converted into alcohol (which has a lower specific gravity than water) and carbon dioxide gas (which escapes as gas).

$$C_6H_{12}O_6 \longrightarrow 2C_2H_5OH + 2CO_2$$

The percentage drop in gravity is measured with a saccharometer and calculated as follows:

Formula: $A = (B - b)/B \times 100$

Example: $(12 - 4)/12 \times 100 = 66.6\%$

A = attenuation: % of sugar of the original wort converted into alcohol and carbon dioxide after or during fermentation

B = original gravity in °Balling (or Plato) prior to fermentation

b = specific gravity in °B (or °P) after or during fermentation.

See also: apparent attenuation; real attenuation; final (degree of) attenuation; primary attenuation; secondary attenuation.

attenuation final. Synonym for final degree of attenuation.

attenuation limit. Synonym for final degree of attenuation.

audit ale. A strong ale formerly brewed at Trinity College, Cambridge, for the day of audit. At Oxford College a similar beer was called brasenose ale.

austere. Synonym for astringent.

autolysis. The process of self-digestion of the body content of a cell by its own enzymes. The slow disintegration and breakdown of the membrane of yeast cells, in the fermenting medium, allows for the passage of nitrogen into the wort. If too pronounced the autolysis process will give a "yeasty" flavor to the finished beer.

automatic carbon dioxide injector. A type of CO_2 injector fitted on pressure barrels and containers to maintain a constant cover of carbon dioxide so as to keep the beer fresh and take up the pressure in the container during use.

awn. Any of the long bristle fibers at the end of glumes on oats, barley and some wheat and grasses or, usually, such fibers collectively. **Syn**: beard. **See also**: glume.

awn-cutter. An machine used in maltings to remove the awns on kilned-dried malted barley.

Bb

B. Abbreviation for Balling (°B).

b-acid. Abbreviated form of beta acid.

B & B. In England, a mix of equal parts of Burton ale and bitter.

baby. In England, a quarter bottle with a capacity, when for beer, of one imperial gill (0.1355 liter).

bacteria. A group of unicellular microorganisms lacking chlorophyl and reproducing rapidly by simple fission. They are classed according to their shape: bacilli (singular: bacillus) are rod-shaped, cocci (singular: coccus) are spherical or ovoid, vibro are comma-shaped and spirillum are curved and rod-like, or on the basis of their oxygen requirements: aerobic bacteria require atmospheric oxygen while anaerobic bacteria cannot live in the presence of oxygen. Bacteria develop under strict conditions of pH (6 to 9), temperature, and humidity (above 90%) and may be killed by disinfectants. They are responsible for the degradation and spoilage of food and for disease.

balché. A type of mead made by the Mayan of the Yucatan Peninsula and mentioned by the explorer Gomara in 1578. It also is the name of a local tree, the *Lonchocarpus longistylus*, from which a bark extract, an alcaloid of the same nature as nicotine, quinine, morphine and caffeine, was prepared and added to the fermenting must, giving it a purgative property. Balché was a sacred drink believed to purify the soul and body. The god of balché was Acon.

Ball. A shot of whiskey chased with a glass of beer.

Balling. 1. A type of saccharometer devised by Carl Joseph Napoleon Balling in 1843. Balling noticed that the extract in wort increased the density of the wort in almost the same proportion as saccharose increases the density of water. He prepared solutions of saccharose and computed tables giving the extract content based on the density of the wort. The Balling saccharometer is graduated in grams per hundred (or percent) so as to give a direct reading of the percentage of extract by weight per 100 grams solution and is calibrated for use at 17.5°C. Example: 10°B = 10 grams of sugar per 100 grams of wort. Pale ales commonly tend to be around 13.5°B, porters around 12.5°B, and stouts 17°B or more. 1°B = 3.8 points on the specific gravity scale. Since the reading gives the percentage extract by weight it must be multiplied by the specific gravity to obtain the percentage weight per 100 milliliters. The tables computed by Balling were slightly erroneous and were corrected by Plato about 1900. Balling also devised the following formula to calculate the original extract of a beer from its alcohol content and terminal (or true) gravity:

$$E = [(2.665 \times A + n) \times 100] / (100 + 1.0665 \times A)$$

E = original extract

n = true extract of the beer

A = percent weight of alcohol

2. Balling (degree). A measure on the Balling saccharometer. Abbrev.: °B. **See also:** Brix; Plato.

Bamberg beer. Synonym for Rauchbier.

Bamberger Rauchbier. Synonym for Rauchbier.

banana ester. Synonym for amyl acetate.

banana oil. Synonym for amyl acetate.

Bang. A mixed drink of warm spiced ale, cider and whiskey.

Bantu beer. Synonym for kaffir beer.

barley. A cereal of the genus *Hordeum*, a member of the *Gramineae* or grass family of plants that also includes wheat, rye, oats, maize, rice, millet and sorghum. There are two varieties of barley classed according to the number of rows of grain on each of the ears of the plant: two- and six-rowed barley. Barley is the cereal grain preferred for brewing because the corn (or grain) is covered by a straw-like husk that protects the embryo (or germ) during malting and helps to filter the wort during lautering by forming a filter bed. The essential qualities for brewing barley are high starch content, sufficient diastatic power to transform the starch into sugar, low protein content, germinative power close to or above 98%. Because carbohydrates, especially starch, constitute the bulk of the extract, a high nitrogen content automatically means a reduced amount of starch and sugars; hence, the higher the nitrogen content of the barley, the lower the extract that can be obtained from its malt. The average weight of the barley grain is 35 mg. Substitute cereal grains used in brewing are called adjuncts.

barley broth. 1. Colloquialism for strong ale. **2.** Whiskey. **Obsolete syn:** barley-bree; barley-broo.

barley-corn. A grain of barley. Also spelled: barleycorn.

barley island. An old English name for an ale-house.

barley wine. 1. Historically, the name given by ancient Egyptians and Greeks to "wine made from barley" which is translated in modern English texts as barley wine. 2. In England, the name given to any top-fermented beer of unusually high, wine-like, alcohol content prepared from worts of 1.065 to 1.120 original gravity yielding about 12% alcohol by volume. Barley wines are usually copper-colored or dark brown, strongly flavored, fruity and bitter-sweet and are sometimes fermented with wine or Champagne yeast. Because of their unusual strength they have little head retention and require long aging periods ranging from six months to many years. They are often brewed for special events. Russian stout, although slightly less alcoholic (10.5% v/v), is classed by many as a barley wine while others consider it to be a style unto itself. Also spelled: barleywine. **See also:** Russian stout.

barm, to. To pitch; i.e., to add yeast.

barm. 1. Liquid yeast appearing as froth on fermenting beer. **Syn:** barm beer. 2. Synonym for brewers' yeast, especially from the strain *Saccharomyces cerevisiae*. 3. The foam on a glass of beer.

barm beer. See: barm.

baron. In Belgium, a beer glass with a capacity of 50 centiliters. **See also:** formidable.

barrel. 1. A large cylindrical container of greater length than breadth and with bulging sides once made of wood coated with tar (pitch) to prevent infection, now made of aluminum or stainless steel. 2. A standard liquid measure: in the U.S. 31 1/2 gallons (119.2369 liter) although Federal tax laws are based on a 31— gallon (117.344 liter) capacity.

1 (full) barrel	=	31 US gallons	=	117.344 liters
1/2 (half) barrel	=	15.5 US gallons	=	58.672 liters
1/4 (quarter) barrel	=	7.75 US gallons	=	29.336 liters
1/8 barrel (or pony)	=	3.875 US gallons	=	14.668 liters

In Britain, a beer barrel has a capacity of 36 imperial gallons (163.65 liter), while an ale barrel has a capacity of 32 imperial gallons (146.472 liter). Abbrev: bbl.

barreling. The action of transferring beer into barrels.

barrique. 1. The French name for a hogshead, the official capacity of which varies with region and commodity. 2. In Britain, a cask containing 50 imperial gallons (227.495 liters).

basi. The traditional alcoholic drink of the Ilocanos of the Philippines prepared by fermenting sugarcane juice and flavored with herbs.

batch fermentation. The traditional method of fermentation where each batch is fermented separately as opposed to continuous fermentation.

Baudelot cooler. A type of wort cooler consisting of a series of horizontal copper pipes laid in a vertical plane activated by cold water or brine. The wort is poured over the pipes and gradually reaches the fermentation temperature of 14 to 25°C (57 to 77°F) for ales and 5 to 12°C (41 to 54°F) for lagers. During this process, the wort acquires the oxygen essential to start fermenting while being particularly exposed to wild yeasts and infections.

Baumé hydrometer. A hydrometer used mainly in France to determine the percentage of alcohol obtainable after complete fermentation in average cellar conditions.

Bavarian Northern Brewer. A seedless variety of hops grown in Bavaria and containing 7% alpha acids. It is more resistant to disease than Hallertauer which is gradually being wiped out by disease.

Bayerischer Weize. See: Weizenbier.

Bayerisches Reinheitsgebot. See: Reinheitsgebot.

B.B. See: B & B.

bbl. Abbreviation for barrel.

bead. 1. The bubbles rising to the surface of a glass of beer. **2.** The ring of bubbles adhering to the glass once the foam collar has collapsed.

beard. Synonym for awn. **See also:** malt tails; malt comes; glume.

beer. 1. A generic name for alcoholic beverages produced by fermenting a cereal or a mixture of cereals. **2.** More specifically, an alcoholic beverage made by fermenting malt with or without other cereals and flavored with hops. Etym: From the Latin *bibere* meaning to drink.

COMPOSITION:		NUTRIENTS: 12 fl.oz.	
Water	75 to 92%	Water	92 %
Alcohol	2 to 13%	Food energy	150 kcal
Albuminoids	3 to 6%	Protein	1.1 g
Dextrins	3 to 6%	Carbohydrate	14 g
Mineral salts	0 to 2%	Calcium	18 mg
Carbon dioxide	0.1 to 0.4%	Sodium	28 mg
		Thiamine	0.01 mg
		Riboflavin	0.11 mg
		Niacin	2.2 mg

beer barrel. 1. In America, a beer barrel has an official capacity of 31 gallons (117.34 liters). **2.** In England, a beer barrel has a capacity of 36 imperial gallons (163.65 liters) while an ale barrel contains 32 imperial gallons (146.47 liters). **See also:** barrel. **3.** Slang for a drunkard.

beer blast. American student slang for a party where large quantities of beer are consumed. **Syn:** beer bust.

beer-brewer. One who brews beer. **See also:** ale-brewer.

beer bust. Synonym for beer blast.

Beer Buster. A mixed drink served in a highball glass consisting of beer, 1 1/2 ounces of vodka and a dash of Tabasco sauce.

beer can. 1. Historically, a pail-like vessel to carry beer from the tavern to the home. **2.** Today, a sealed aluminum container in which beer is sold with a capacity, in the U.S., of 12 fluid ounces (355 ml), sometimes 1/3 larger (1 pint) or 1/2 smaller.

beer engine. A pump-like tap for drawing beer from the cask or cellar to the bar. **Syn:** beer pump. **See also:** beer-pull.

beer festivals. See: Adriaan Brouwer Bierfesten, Bergkirchweih, Canstatter Wasen, Carnaval de Binche, Frühjahrsbierfest, Kermesse de la bière de Maubeuge (Julifest Maubergeoise), Leuven Bier Festival, Oktoberfest, Poperinge Hoppefeesten, Wieze Oktoberfesten.

beer from the wood. Draft beer.

beer garden. A terrace area adjoining a tavern where beer is served. Sometimes called: beer hall. A term and tradition borrowed from Germany where it is called Biergarten, or Bierkeller if the beer casks are kept in a cellar. There are more than one hundred beer gardens in München alone and the largest, Hirschgarten, can seat 7,000 people.

beer gardener. Slang name for a beer garden owner.

beer hall. 1. See also: beer garden. **2.** A large room in an establishment where only beer is sold.

beer-house. A place licensed to sell beer only.

beer jug. A name given by antique dealers and collectors to a type of 18th century glass engraved with hops and/or barley with a capacity of approximately one quart. **Syn:** ale jug.

beer house. In England, a public house where only malt liquors are sold. Also spelled: beerhouse.

beer life. Synonym for shelf life.

beer on tap. Draft beer. **Syn:** beer from the wood.

beer parlor. In Canada, an establishment where only malt liquors are sold.

beer-pull. The handle of a beer-engine.

beer pump. Synonym for beer engine.

beer saloon. In pre-Prohibition America, an establishment where draft beer was sold.

beer scale. Synonym for beerstone.

beer stein. A cylindrical or slightly tapering ceramic mug usually covered with a hinged metal lid. **See also**: stein.

beerstone. Technically, calcium oxylate acid which is precipitated by the addition of calcium. In homebrewing, beerstone is evident when the same vessel is used repeatedly; a hard film forms through the combination of calcium oxylate, protein and sugar. Also spelled: beer stone. **Syn**: beer scale.

Beer-Wine Revenue Act. Another name for the Cullen Act.

beery. Pertaining to beer or resembling it in taste, aroma or composition.

bees wine. An obsolete name for mead.

beet sugar. Sucrose obtained from sugarbeet.

Belgian degree. In Belgium, the density of the wort is derived from the value of the specific gravity by subtracting 1 and moving the decimal point two digits to the right. Hence, a specific gravity of 1.069 = 6.9° Belgian. 1° Belgian equals approximately 2.5° Plato.

belied measure. An early English baluster-shaped ale measure.

bentonite. A clay mined in the U.S., natural aluminum silicate of the monmorillonite group, used industrially at a rate of 20 to 60 grams per hectoliter to clarify beer through the adsorption of colloidal substances. The contact period must not be too long because bentonite affects foam retention and taste. On the other hand, if too short, the treatment is ineffective. **Obsolete syn**: Wyoming clay.

Bergkirchweih. A beer festival held annually during Whitsuntide in Erlangen, Franconia (Germany).

Berliner Weisse. A regional beer of northern Germany, principally Berlin; a very pale (but not white) top-fermented beer of low-density (7 to 8°B) made from a one-to-three or -four wheat-to-barley ratio. It is lightly hopped and mildly alcoholic at 2 to 3% alcohol by weight (2.5 to 3.7% v/v). A secondary fermentation induced by the addition of a lactic acid culture (Lactobacillus, sour milk) at 20°C (68°F) is responsible for its dry, sharp flavor, its thick white foam and the deposit of yeast in the bottle. It is traditionally served in large, bowl-shaped stemglasses with a dash of green essence of woodruff or red raspberry syrup (*Schulthies Berliner Weisse* and *Kindel Berliner Weisse*). Its popularity dates back to Imperial Germany but it is mentioned in texts as early as 1572. It is also known as Champagne of the Spree and was nicknamed *Champagne du Nord* by Napoleon's troops. **Syn**: Weissbier or weisse Bier. **See also**: wheat beer; Weissbier; Weizenbier.

Berliner Weisse mit Strippe. Berliner Weisse served in a tall glass with a proportionately tall head and accompanied by a chaser of Kummel spirits in a smaller glass.

Berliner Weisse mit Schuss. Berliner Weisse served in a tall glass to which is added a little raspberry syrup.

best bitter. Bitter ale prepared from an original wort gravity of 1.035 to 1.040. It tends to be medium-bodied, dry and hoppy. **See also:** bitter.

beta acid. One of the two resins in hops; it consists of a mixture of three closely related chemical compounds — lupulone, colupulone and adlupulone. Contrary to alpha acid, it contributes very little (1/10) to the bitterness of beer and accounts for approximately one-third of its preservative quality. Beta acids comprise about 25% of soft resins. They are present in larger quantities than alpha acids but because of their low solubility (soluble in water only if oxidized) their content level is usually insignificant. Abbrev: b-acid. **Syn:** lupulon(e); beta resin. **See also:** alpha acid; soft resin; lupulin.

beta-amylase. A diastatic enzyme produced by malting barley, also known as saccharifying enzyme because it converts dextrins and soluble starches into maltose, maltotriose, glucose and limit dextrins. Beta amylases work best at low pH (± 5.0 to 5.2) and at temperatures ranging from 57 to 66°C (135 to 150°F) and is destroyed at 75°C (167°F). **Syn:** beta resin; saccharifying enzyme; maltogenic amylase. **See also:** amylase; alpha amylase.

beta resin. Synonym for beta acid.

bevel. The outer surface at the head of a cask or barrel.

beverage. 1. Any potable liquid. **2.** More often applied to an artificially prepared drink of pleasant taste and odor.

beverage(d) alcohol. 1. The ethyl alcohol content of a beverage. **2.** Synonym for alcoholic beverage.

bicarbonate. A salt formed by neutralization of one hydrogen in carbonic acid. Calcium bicarbonate is used in the treatment of water to render it hard.

Bier. German for beer. German beers are classed in three legal categories: **1.** Starkbiers are brewed from an original gravity of 16°B or more and contain at least 5% alcohol by weight (6.2% v/v), **2.** Vollbiers are medium strength beers prepared from original gravities of 11 to 14°B and contain 3.5 to 4.5% alcohol by weight (4.4 to 5.65% v/v), **3.** Schankbiers are brewed from original gravities of 7 to 8°B and contain 2 to 3% alcohol by weight (2.5 to 3.7% v/v).

Bierbauch. German for beer-belly.

bière. French for beer. **1.** French legislation distinguishes three categories of beers based on the original gravity of the wort expressed in *degrés Régie* (°R): *bière de table*, 2.0° to 2.2°R; *bière bock*, 3.3° to 3.9°R; and *bière de luxe*, 4.4°R or higher. The latter category also comprises, since 1971, two subcategories: *bière de choix* (4.4 to 4.6°R) and *bière spéciale* (5.0 to 7.0°R). The term *petite bière* (small beer) refers to low alcoholic beers brewed from an original gravity of 2.0°R or less. **See also:** *Régie.* **2.** In Belgium, there are, since 1974, four legal categories for beer based on the original gravity expressed in degrees Plato (°P): Catégorie S: 15°P or higher; Catégorie I: 11.0 to 13.5°P; Catégorie II: 7.0

to 9.0°P; Catégorie III: 1.0 to 4.0°P. **See also:** *Belgian degree.* Etym: The earliest mention of this word dates back to 1345 in a legal document signed by King Jean le Bon to regulate the trade rules and prices of beer; it occurs again in 1489 in a decree signed by Charles VIII concerning the *Corporation des Brasseurs de Paris.*

bière blanche de Hoegaarden. See: blanche de Hoegaarden.

bière bock. In France, one of the three legal categories for beers comprising those prepared from medium gravity worts of 3.3 to 3.9° Régie. It should not be confused with German bock beers which are strong beers brewed from a wort of 16°P (about 6.5°Régie). **See also:** bière; bock.

bière d'abbaye. French for abbey beer.

bière de couvent. See: bière des pères.

bière de Diest. A very dark, sweet, highly nutritious beer brewed in Belgium from a mix of barley, caramelized malt and 30% wheat. It contains 511 calories per liter as opposed to 400 calories in ordinary beers. **Syn:** Gildenbier.

bière de garde. 1. Generally speaking, any beer that has matured in casks for a long period of time. **2.** More specifically, a regional style of beers from the north of France, so named because they spend long aging periods in casks. These amber-colored beers of 4.4 to 4.8% alcohol by weight (5.5 to 6.0% by volume) are produced by top fermentation to (occasionally by bottom fermentation) from a blend of pale and dark malts in a single-mash system and are sold in corked and wired Champagne-like bottles.

bière de luxe. In France, the legal nomenclature for beers, based on the specific gravity of the original wort expressed in *degrés Régie*, stipulates that the strongest beers (*bière de luxe*) must be brewed from original wort gravities of 4.4°R or higher. **See also:** bière; Régie.

bière de malt. A rich-flavored, low-alcoholic malt beverage once given to children and nursing mothers. It was brewed by adding malt extract to the wort followed by a very light fermentation. **Syn:** *bière de nourrice.* **See also:** malt beer; Malzbier.

bière de mars. A special beer brewed in France by a few breweries to renew with the traditional practice of March beers. Before the advent of artificial cold (end of the 19th century), it was in March that beer was at its best. The barley had been harvested in August, malted in November, brewed in December and lagered until March. **See also:** *Märzenbier.*

bière de moine. French for abbey beer.

bière de nourrice. Synonym for *bière de malt.*

bière des pères. A strong monastery beer brewed in France in the 16th century; a weaker brew was called *bière de couvent.*

bière de table. In France, the legal nomenclature for beers stipulates that low strength table beers must be prepared from original wort gravities of 2.0 to 2.2° Régie. **See also:** *bière.*

Bierkieser. The name given in Alsace in 1723 and 1763 to sworn beer essayers. The role of these experts consisted in tasting the newly tapped beer to ensure that its quality was up to the standards set by the magistrate of that city, who had decreed that only malt, water and hops could be used for its production. The addition of any other ingredients was a punishable offense. In the neighboring regions of Artois and Flanders, people with similar functions were called *eswarts, égards,* or *coeuriers.*

Big Six. Refers to Britain's six largest brewing companies: Courage, Allied Breweries, Scottish & Newcastle, Watneys, Bass Charington and Whitbread. The Big Six produce more than 80% of all the beer sold in Britain and own more than half of all the outlets.

bi-kal. The name given to a heavy beer in ancient Sumeria.

bilbil. A type of beer once brewed in Upper Egypt from durra(h), a type of sorghum also known as Indian millet. The durrah grains were germinated between leaves of onna oskur (*Calotropis procera*), sundried and milled into a fine flour. The flour was mixed with water in large earthenware pots and the wort was boiled for six to eight hours over open fires. After cooling a yeasty preparation was added to induce fermentation. This first brew was called merissa which, if boiled a second time, filtered and refermented was called bilbil. Etym: From bülbül, mother of the nightingale, because it caused drinking men to sing. **Syn:** omm bilbil.

bilge. The wide, bulging part of a cask or barrel located in the middle where the circumference is greatest. Once called: bouge.

bilge-water. British slang for an inferior beer.

billet. Synonym for thumbpiece.

bine. Synonym for hop bine.

biochemical pathway. A sequence of chemical reactions each of which is catalyzed by an enzymes supplied by micro organisms. **See also:** chemical pathway.

biochips. Sterilized sawdust sprayed with pitch and used to assist clarification during secondary fermentation or maturation.

birch beer. A non-alcoholic, usually carbonated, beverage flavored with oils of wintergreen, sweet birch or sassafras.

bi-se-bar. The name given to a light barley beer in ancient Sumeria.

Bismark. The German name given to a mix of Champagne and stout called Black Velvet in the United Kingdom.

bit-sikari. The name given to a brewhouse in ancient Sumeria.

bitter. A sharp and tangy taste in beer associated with hops.

bitter. In Britain, the draft equivalent of pale ale, a golden-brown or copper-colored top-fermented beer usually highly hopped, dry and lightly carbonated. Bitter accounts for about 80% of draft beer sales in English pubs. It is slightly more alcoholic (3.0 to 5.5% v/v) and more heavily hopped than mild (with which it is sometimes mixed). It is usually available in three strengths although there are regional variations: ordinary bitter; OG 1.035 to1.040; best bitter, OG 1.040 to1.048, and special or strong bitter, OG 1.055 to1.065. Traditionally, bitter is unpasteurized and cask-conditioned in the pub cellar. In the 1960s the large brewing companies introduced kegged-beer, a filtered, pasteurized, chilled and artificially carbonated bitter. A consumer campaign initiated by CAMRA (q.v.) in the 1970s opposed this new trend, and naturally conditioned casked bitter is again available as Real Ale. **Obsolete syn:** slight beer. **Syn:** bitter beer; bitter ale. **See also:** ordinary bitter; best bitter; special bitter.

bitter ale. Synonym for bitter.

bittering hops. Synonym for flavoring hops.

bittering units. A formula devised by the American Homebrewers Association to measure the total amount of bitterness in a given volume of beer multiplying the alpha acid content (in percent) by the number of ounces. Example: 2 ounces of hops at 9% alpha acid for five gallons: 2 x 9 = 18 B.U. per 5 gallons. **See also:** bitterness units; homebrewers bittering units; hop bitterness units; hop bitterness coefficient; alpha acids units.

bittern A very bitter mixture of equal parts of quassia and other drugs formerly used for adulterating beer. Ross-Mackenzie (*Brewing and Malting*, London, 1935, p. 163) gives the following formula: equal parts of quassia extract and sulphate of iron, two parts of extract of *cocculus indicus*, eight parts of treacle, and five parts of Spanish juice.

bitterness. The quality or state of being bitter. In beer, the bitter flavor and aroma are caused by the tannins and the isohumulones of hops. When tasting beer a distinction is made between the first bitterness, when the liquid touches the tastebuds, and the post-bitterness felt at the back of the mouth when the beer is swallowed. **See also:** alpha acid; beta acid.

bitterness units. An international system of units for measuring and expressing the bitterness in beer based on the parts per million content (or milligrams per liter) of alpha acids.
Note: this formula is an approximation that can be off by as much as 20%, depending on hop utilization in kettle and isoalpha acid loss during fermentation and aging.
Formula: $B.U. = H \times (a\% + b\% / 9) / 0.3$
Where:

H = weight of hops in grams per liter (H g/l)
a% = alpha acid percent
b% = beta acid percent
9 = a constant. Wöllmer (*Tageszeitung für Brauerei*, 1932) found that the flavoring power of alpha acids was about nine times greater than that of beta acids.
0.3 = a constant which represents an approximate 30% rate of efficiency in hop extraction caused by vaporization or precipitation (boiling, skimming, racking and fining).

Conversely, to calculate the amount of hops in grams per liter required to obtain a specific bitterness unit, the formula is rearranged:

H g/l = (B.U.) / (a% + b% / 9) x 0.3

Example: If a beer is to reach 25 B.U. using Hallertauer hops containing 5% alpha/beta acids: H = (25 / 5) x 0.3 = 1.5 grams per liter (g/l).

Abbrev: B.U. **Syn**: units of bitterness; International Bitterness Unit (I.B.U.). **See also**: alpha acid units; homebrewers bittering units; hop bitterness units; hop bitterness coefficient; bittering units.

bitter resins. Synonym for soft resins.

bitter stout. See: stout.

bitter wort. Sweet wort made bitter by boiling with hops for one to two hours. Boiling extracts and dissolves the bitter resins and aromatic oils contained in the hops in the wort giving it its characteristic bitterness.

black beer. 1. A general term for very dark colored beers. **2.** Synonym for spruce beer.

Black and Tan. A mix of equal parts of dark and pale beers such as porter and Pilsener, stout and mild, or stout and bitter.

Black Champagne. The name given to imported English ale under Louis XIV. According to historians, a rich brewer named Humphrey Parsons, twice mayor of London, visited the French court of Louis XIV. During a steeplechase he accidentally dropped the reins of his black horse, which had the impudence to overrun the King's mount. Upon inquiring as to the identity of the culprit, the King was told that Lord Parsons was a *Chevalier de Malte* and a brewer. Lord Parsons had the diplomatic sense of giving the horse to Louis who in turn asked the brewer to provide the Court of Versailles with his stout, which the courtiers called Black Champagne.

Black Jack. A large tankard-like drinking vessel made of leather internally water-proofed with black pitch or resin common in England in the 16th and 17th centuries. Also spelled: black jack; blackjack.

black malt. Partly malted barley of moderate nitrogen content (1.5%), germinated for 4 to 6 days and kiln-dried down to 2 to 5% moisture and then roasted at high temperature (±232°C, 450°F) for 2 to 2 1/2 hours in a coke or gas-heated rotating drum. It is used in small amounts in stouts and dark beers to which it contributes a dark color and a burnt or carbonized flavor. Since it contains no fermentable sugar, all the solids extracted from it remain in the finished beer. **Syn**: black patent malt; patent malt; carbonized malt; chocolate malt. **See also**: chocolate malt.

black mead. A variety of melomel prepared by fermenting a must of honey, black currant and water.

Black Velvet. A cocktail mix of equal parts of stout and Champagne (or sparkling wine) usually prepared in a Champagne glass by slowly pouring the stout on the side of the glass so that it does not mix with the Champagne. **See also**: Bismark.

blanche de Hoegaarden. A traditional wheat beer brewed in one of the oldest and once the largest brewing town of Flanders in Belgium (30 breweries for 2000 people in 1745). It is stated in an old document that "in Hoegaarden, only animals drink water." The *bière blanche* is prepared from a mash of 50% barley malt and 50% wheat, sometimes with the addition of 10% oats (or oat flakes). Originally, it was fermented by wild yeasts and lactic bacteria and sold to wholesalers only a few days after primary fermentation, or it was buried in March to be unearthed the following year and was then an occasion for celebrations. The brewery, closed in the 1950s after 500 years of operation, was reopened in the 1960s by a Monsieur Celis, and this style of beer is once again brewed by top fermentation in aluminum vats. **Syn**: Hoegaardse Wit.

blanche de Louvain. A traditional, top-fermented wheat beer brewed in the Flemish town of Louvain in Belgium. The mashing process, from a mix of malt and raw wheat in a ratio of 60:40, 50:50, or 45:45 with 10% oats, is very long, up to 17 hours, and only about one third of the wort is boiled with hops. The original wort density ranges from 1.040 to 1.048 (4.0 to 4.8°Belgian). **Syn**: Leuvense Wit.

blend, to. To mix together products of the same nature or varieties of the same product.

blend. A product obtained by mixing substances of the same nature.

blending. The action of mixing together two or more products of the same nature.

blind pig. During Prohibition, an illegal drinking saloon. The term originated in Maine in the 1850s when saloon-owners attempted to evade the prohibitory law of that state by charging admission to view a "blind pig" which entitled the customer to a free drink. **Syn**: blind tiger.

blood heat. An empirical method of ascertaining or expressing the temperature of a liquid by dipping a finger or an elbow, which should feel neither hot nor cold. In homebrewing this constitutes a test to determine the appropriate time for pitching the yeast. **Syn**: blood temperature; blood warm.

blow-by. In homebrewing, a single-stage fermentation method using a glass or plastic carboy into the mouth of which a plastic hose is fitted, curving down over the edge into a pail of sterile water. This method allows the primary fermentation to blow-out all the froth and carbon dioxide while preventing air coming into contact with the fermenting beer, thus avoiding contamination. After one to three days the beer is either transferred to a second carboy or left in the first one for the secondary fermentation process.

blow-out tube. A one-inch plastic tube fitted into the mouth of a carboy in the blow-by method.

Bock(bier). 1. A very strong beer originally brewed by top fermentation in the Hanseatic League town of Einbeck in Lower Saxony where it is still brewed and known as Ur-Bock, the original bock. It was once a heavy dark beer brewed in winter for consumption in spring. German bock beers are now brewed by bottom fermentation and are usually dark brown, but pale bocks are increasing in popularity and a distinction is sometimes made between "light bock beer" and "dark bock beer." Modern bockbiers, according to German law, must be fermented from an original wort gravity of at least 16°P (1.064) resulting in an alcoholic content of 6% by weight or higher (7.5% v/v). They are full-bodied, malty and well-hopped. Etym: From the town of Einbeck (ca 1250) in northern Germany. This beer was later exported to München and was one of the first beers to be brewed by the Hofbraü, the brewery of the dukes of Bavaria. In the 18th century, the name became Oanbock and was later shortened to bock. According to one legend, bock was once made from the dregs of barrels and vats at spring cleaning. This is obviously untrue since such a beer would have been weak, to say the least. Since the word bock also means male goat or Billy goat in German, such an animal is often represented on the labels of bottles containing bockbier. **See also:** Doppelbock; Eisbock. 2. In America, bock beers made their first appearance around 1840 and were seasonal beers available at springtime. After Prohibition was repealed (Dec. 1933), bars proclaimed the good news with a sign saying "Bock is back," but in fact the sales of bock beers dwindled and production was discontinued until the 1970s when a few bock beers were revived. American bock beers are usually light-bodied and mildly-hopped. The name of these so-called bock beers comes not from their strength but rather from their dark color and artificial flavoring (caramel). 3. In France, bock refers to a medium strength beer of medium density ranging from 3.3° to 3.9° Régie. **See also:** bière bock. 4. In France, a beer glass with a capacity of either 33 centiliters or 1/4 of a liter (25 cl).

body. The consistency, thickness and mouth-filling property of a beer. The sensation of palate fullness in the mouth ranges from full-bodied to thin-bodied. Lack of body is the opposite. **Syn:** mouth-feel or mouthfeel; fullness.

boiler. A large vessel in which to boil the wort.

boiler hopping. The addition of finishing hops near the end of the boiling process or 10 to 30 minutes after boiling has stopped for the purpose of increasing the aromatic character of the finished beer.

Boilermaker. 1. A jigger of whiskey chased with a glass of beer. Etym: The word apparently comes from the expression "head of steam" used to describe the heady feeling that this drink generates. **2.** Sometimes, salted beer.

boiling. An operation that in transfers the sweet wort to the brew kettle (or copper) for boiling for one to two and a half hours. During that time, flavoring (or bittering) hops will be added at the beginning of the process and finishing (or aromatic) hops will be added near the end to produce the bitter wort. The objective of boiling is to stabilize the composition of the final wort, to clarify it through the coagulation and precipitation of tannins and proteins, to sterilize it by killing bacteria, and to extract the desirable principals of the hops that give beer its characteristic flavor and aroma. Boiling also contributes to the color through the caramelization of sugars and the formation of melanoidins. At the end of the boiling stage the hops are removed and the wort is quickly cooled to further clarify the brew. **Syn:** brewing.

boiling copper. Synonym for brew-kettle.

boiling hops. Synonym for flavoring hops.

boggle. A pitcher- or jug-like drinking vessel of Scottish origin shaped in the likeness of a man.

bolt, to. **1.** Synonym for to sieve. **2.** In British maltings, the term refers exclusively to separating the flour from the products of grinding.

booza(h). Orthographic variant for boza.

botte. A French beer glass with a capacity of one liter. **See also:** demi; lion; distingué.

bottle. A glass container with a narrow neck for holding liquids.

bottle-aged. Synonym for bottle-conditioned.

bottle-capper. See: capper.

bottle-conditioned. **1.** Said of a beer aged in the bottle. **Syn:** bottle-aged. **2.** Said of a beer carbonated naturally by priming or re-yeasting. **See also:** conditioning; carbonation.

bottled beer. Beer sold in bottles as opposed to casked or canned beer. Bottled beer is frequently chilled, filtered, carbonated, pasteurized, and sterilized by the addition of inhibitory materials.

bottled draft beer. A mislabeled product consisting, like draft, of unpasteurized beer.

bottled-goods. Alcoholic beverages sold in bottles.

bottled mild. Synonym for brown ale.

bottle opener. A device for levering (prying-off) bottle caps.

bottle pressure. American brewers bottle beer at about 2.5 atmospheric pressure (±37 lbs/in² or 2.58 kg/cm²). Bottle pressure at a given CO_2 level varies dramatically with temperature. For example, if a beer contains 2.5 volumes of CO_2, then a bottle pressure of 37 psi will occur at 79 F; however, at 45 F the pressure will be approximately 15 psi. Homebrewers can produce such pressure by priming with 1.5 ounces of dextrose per gallon of beer (1.8 oz per imperial gallon) prior to bottling. **Syn:** bottling pressure.

bottlery. Synonym for bottling department.

bottle-washer. An automatic machine for washing bottles.

bottle-works. Synonym for bottling department.

bottling. The action of filling bottles manually or automatically. Because bottled beer is often stored for longer periods and at warmer temperatures than draft beer, it is usually pasteurized to prevent any further fermentation.

bottling department. The area of the brewery where bottles are washed, sterilized, filled, capped, labeled and packaged. **Syn:** bottlery; bottling hall; bottle-works.

bottling fleet. The total amount of bottles owned by a brewery.

bottling hall. Synonym for bottling department.

bottling line. An automated U- or L-shaped production line where bottles are examined, washed, rinsed, sterilized, filled, labelled and corked.

bottling pressure. Synonym for bottle pressure.

bottom fermentation. One of the two basic methods of fermentation for beer, characterized by the fact that dead yeast cells sink to the bottom during fermentation. The maximum growth temperature for Saccharomyces carlsbergensis is 31.6 to 34.0°C (88.9 to 93.2°F). Primary fermentation requires temperatures of 5 to 10°C (41 to 50°F) usually over a cycle of 5 to 9 to 5°C or 7 to 12 to 7°C (41 to 48 to 41°F or 45 to 54 to 45°F), and secondary fermentation takes place at close to 0°C (1 to 2°C, 34 to 36°F). Beers brewed in this fashion are commonly called lagers or bottom-fermented beers.

bottom fermentation yeast. Synonym for bottom fermenting yeast.

bottom-fermented beer. Synonym for lager.

bottom fermenting lager yeast. Synonym for bottom fermenting yeast.

bottom fermenting yeast. One of the two types of brewers' yeast so named because the majority of the yeast cells flocculate and sink to the bottom of the wort toward the end of fermentation. Lager yeasts work best at 5 to 10°C (41 to 50°F) but can ferment at temperatures as low as 1°C (34°F) and they have the ability to ferment melibiose sugar because of the presence of melibiase enzymes in their cells. Lager yeast is thought to have been first isolated by a German monk named Benno Scharl, who operated a small brewery near

Munich around 1810. It was later used by the Spatenbrauerei (Spaten brewery). Samples of this yeast were taken from Munich to Copenhagen by Jacob Christian Jacobsen in 1845-46, a 500-mile journey by stage-coach. Here they were analyzed by the microbiologist Emil Hanses of the Carlsberg labs, who isolated the first single-cell culture of this yeast which he named Saccharomyces carlsbergensis. **Syn:** Saccharomyces carlsbergensis; Saccharomyces uvarum; lager yeast; bottom-fermenting lager yeast; bottom fermentation yeast; bottom yeast.

bottoms. Yeast sediments that have collected at the bottom of a fermentation vessel or conditioning tank.

bouge. An obsolete synonym for bilge.

bouquet. The overall smell of beer caused by odors that originate during fermentation and maturation. **See also:** aroma.

boutique brewery. A small brewery with a production of less than 15,000 barrels per year.

box malting. A type of pneumatic malting process carried out in germination boxes. **Syn:** compartment malting.

boza. 1. In ancient Babylonia and Egypt (3000 to 2000 BC), a type of beer usually fermented from millet (*Panicum miliaceum*). Until recently, an archaic method of preparing boza, practiced by desert nomads (fellaheen), was steeping and partially germinating millet. Afterward, the grains were crushed into a dough and baked into dehydrated cake-like masses. Once in the desert, the cakes where broken into pieces, steeped in water and fermented. 2. In Ethiopia, a wheat beer. 3. In Turkey, a non-alcoholic beer prepared from corn. Also spelled: bosa; bousa; bouza; booza(h). The term "booze" is probably derived from booza.

bousa. Orthographic variant for boza.

bracteole. Any of the overlapping petals which constitute the strobile (hop cone). **Syn:** breact.

braga. 1. A mild mead made in Russia in the Middle Ages. 2. Romanian millet beer.

bragget. Honey-sweetened spiced ale or a mix of mead and ale. Etym: Because it was drunk ceremoniously on Bragget Sunday, the fourth Sunday in Lent, in 19th century England.

bragot. An ancient Welsh drink consisting of beer, honey, cinnamon and "galingale." It also was known as heroe drink.

brasenose ale. Synonym for audit ale.

brassage. From *brace*, grain used to prepare malt and *bracis*, steeped, softened grain.

brasserie. A bar where food and drink are served. From *brasser*, to brew. **See**

also: brassage.

breact. Synonym for bracteole.

break. The coagulation and precipitation of protein matter during the boiling stage (hot break) and cooling stage (cold break).

breakage. Synonym for flocculation.

Brettanomyces. A genus of the *Fungi imperfecti* class of yeasts. It is used in Belgium for brewing lambic beers. It produces more esters than other yeasts and imparts a characteristic fruity aroma to beer.

brew, to. 1. Generally speaking, to make beer. **2.** More specifically, the infusion and boiling stages of the beermaking process; i.e., preparing the bitter wort.

brew. 1. Synonym for beer. **2.** The wort (or the quantity of it) in preparation.

brewer. A person or industrialist who makes beer. Etym: From the Gallic word *brai* (or *brace*) originally meaning barley, and later barley mixed with water. **See also:** master-brewer.

breweress. Synonym for brewster.

breweriana. The collecting of beer-related artifacts by enthusiasts.

Brewer's Gold. A variety of hops cultivated in Kent, England and in Washington and Oregon in the U.S. containing 8.5 to 11% alpha acids and 4.5 to 5.5% beta acids.

brewers' grains. Synonym for spent grains.

brewer's gravity. Specific gravity in brewer's pounds. Formula: (S.G. - 1000) x 0.36. **See also:** brewer's pounds.

brewers' grits. Coarsely crushed barley, corn, or rice grains that have to be treated in a converter prior to mashing.

brewer's paddle. A long-handled wooden or polypropylene paddle-like instrument used to stir (or rouse) the beer at various stages of production. **Syn:** rouser; stirring spoon.

brewer's pounds. The excess weight of a barrel (36 imperial gallons) of wort over that of a barrel of water (360 pounds) at 60°F (15.5°C). This figure represents the extract in brewer's pounds. Hence, the specific gravity of the wort is calculated by the following formula: (excess brewer's pounds + 360)/ 360. **See also:** extract; brewer's gravity.

brewer's yeast. Yeast specifically prepared for beer brewing. Two main types of yeast are used for beer making: one ferments at the top of the brew (top fermenting yeast) and the other ferments at the bottom (bottom fermenting yeast). Brewer's yeast may be gathered from the lees of the previous brew or it may be purchased in dry or liquid form. **Syn:** brewing yeast.

brewery. 1. A building in which beer is made. **2.** A place were beer is served.

brewhouse. 1. An obsolete synonym for brewery. **2.** The section of a brewery where the actual brewing or mashing takes place. Also spelled: brew-house.

brewing. 1. The art (or science) of making beer. Commercial brewing is divided into nine basic steps: steeping, germinating, kilning, milling, mashing, lautering, boiling, fermenting, and bottling (canning or casking). All nine stages can be accomplished in two weeks to four months. **2.** More specifically, the mashing and boiling stages. **3.** Pertaining to the beer-making process.

brewing copper. Synonym for brew kettle.

brewing liquor. Synonym for brewing water.

brewing water. For centuries, breweries were located near wells that supplied water of suitable quality and quantity. Some brewing centers became famous for their particular type of beer and the individual flavors of their beer were strongly influenced by the brewing water used. Burton is renowned for its bitter beers, Edinburgh for its pale ales, Dortmund for its pale lager and Plzeň for its Pilsner Urquell, also a pale lager. **Syn:** liquor; brewing liquor.

Ionic Concentrations of Salts in Typical Brewing Liquors (in millivals*)						
Ions	**Burton†**	**Edin-burgh**	**London†**	**Dort-mund**	**Munich**	**Plzen**
Sodium	1.3	4.0	4.3	3.0	0.1	0.1
Magnesium	5.2	3.0	1.6	1.9	1.6	0.1
Calcium	13.4	7.0	2.6	13.0	4.0	0.4
Nitrate	0.5	0.5	-	-	0.1	-
Chloride	1.0	1.7	1.7	3.0	0.1	0.1
Sulfate	13.7	4.8	1.6	5.9	0.1	0.1
Carbonate	4.7	7.0	5.2	9.0	5.5	0.3
Total salts (ppm)	1226	800	463	1011	273	30.8

* Millivals are the equivalent weight in milligrams per liter, or N/1000, or 0.001 Normal. 1 millival = 1 mg equivalent per liter. Water with less than 2.5 millivals is considered soft; 2.5 to 5.0 is moderately soft; 5.0 to 7.5 is slightly hard; 7.5 to 12.5 is moderately hard; 12.5 to 17.5 is hard; above 12.5 is very hard.
† Burton = Burton-on-Trent. London = deep-well water.

brewing yeast. Synonym for brewer's yeast.

brew kettle. A large vessel, similar in shape to a mash tun, made of copper or stainless steel and into which the wort is heated for one to two hours by direct flame, by means of steam coils or through a jacketed bottom, and is surmounted by a chimney for the evacuation of steam. Copper is the metal preferred for its manufacture because it has three times the heat conductibility of stainless steel. On the other hand, copper affects the colloidal stability of beer because it acts as a catalyst for oxidation. In Great Britain the term "copper" is preferred. **Syn:** brewing copper; copper; kettle; brewpot; wort kettle; wort boiler; wort copper.

brewmaster. Synonym for master-brewer.

brewpot. Synonym for brew kettle.

brewster. 1. A female brewer. 2. Synonym for ale-wife.

Brewster Sessions. In old England, by a law of 1729, special sessions of the Justice of the Peace to consider the issue or renewal of licenses to operate ale-houses.

bridal. See: bride ale.

bride ale. In old England, a wedding feast where the bride prepared a special batch of her finest ale for friends and attendants who contributed money according to their purse. The tradition dates back to the Middle Ages and the words bridal and bridale were derived from it.

bright. 1. Synonym for brilliant. 2. Effervescent.

brilliance. An expression of the quality of beer in terms of clearness, limpidity, brightness and sparkle. To retain its brilliance a beer must have good biological and colloidal stability. Sometimes called: purity; brilliancy.

brilliancy. Synonym for brilliance.

brilliant. Is said of a beer showing good clarity, brightness and sparkling qualities. **Syn:** bright.

brim. The upper edge of a cup, bowl or plate.

brine. An aqueous solution of calcium chloride or sodium chloride used in the brewing industry as a freezing medium in coolers and refrigerators. **Syn:** saltwater or salt-water.

British Champagne. A sobriquet for porter.

Brix. A specific gravity scale based on the Balling scale but designed for use at 15°C (59°F).

broach, to. To insert a tap in a cask for the purpose of drawing its contents.

broc. An old French capacity measure for liquids.

bromelain. An enzyme that breaks down protein. It is prepared by the precipitation of pineapple juice by acetone for use in the brewing industry as a chill-proofing agent. Also spelled: bromelin.

bromelin. An orthographic variant of bromelain.

brother bung. British slang for a brewer or a drinking partner.

brown ale. In Britain, a dark-colored top-fermented beer considered by many as the bottled equivalent of mild ale, although it is somewhat sweeter and fuller bodied. Brown ales are lightly hopped and are flavored and colored with roasted and caramel malts. They are brewed with soft water from original wort gravities ranging from 1.035 to 1.050 resulting in an alcohol content of about 3.5% or more. Sometimes called: bottled mild.

brown beer. A general name for dark-hued, slightly coppery beers. **See also:** brown ale; brune d'Aarschot.

Brown Betty. In old England, a hot or warm drink of brandy and ale served with spiced toasts.

brown cow. British slang for a cask of ale.

Brown Velvet. A mix of equal parts of stout and port.

brown water. Australian slang for beer.

Bruheater. Trade name for a multipurpose wort boiler, masher and sparger thermostatically-controlled by rheostat. It was invented in England, has a six-gallon capacity and is designed for a single infusion mash at 71°C (160°F).

brumalis canna. A foamy aromatic beer made from ginger and fruit in medieval France.

brumalt. A very dark, sugar-rich malt prepared in Europe from highly steeped, 8-day malt placed under a cover in layers of 20 cm for 24 hours causing the temperature to rise sharply to about 50°C (122°F) where it levels briefly and then drops sharply when the oxygen under the cover is consumed and carbon dioxide starts to accumulate. This is followed by kilning at temperatures of no more than 100°C (212°F).

brune d'Aarschot. A brown beer once brewed in Belgium from a mix of 60% malt and 40% wheat, flavored with old hops and fermented in large, 230-liter vats, called Poensels.

brush, to. To clean mechanically the surface of barley grains by means of a brush.

brutolé. A medicinal beer once brewed by dissolving medicinal or curative herbs and spices into beer. For example, an Egyptian prescription dated 1600 BC recommends mixing half an onion with beer foam to guard against death.

bubbler. Synonym for fermentation lock, so named because of the bubbles of carbon dioxide gas rising in the water-filled lock.

budding. The most common form of yeast cell reproduction. The cell increases in size forming a rounded outgrowth that eventually separates into a daughter cell.

buire. An old French drinking vessel similar in shape to a flagon.

Bullion. A variety of very bitter hops grown in England and in Washington and Oregon in the U.S. containing 8.5 to 11% alpha acids and 4.5 to 5.5% beta acids.

bung, to. To plug the bung-hole of a cask hermetically, thus preventing carbon dioxide gas from escaping and allowing the beer to saturate naturally. A safety valve is sometimes used for this purpose to ensure a maximum pressure of 300 grams per square centimeter.

bung. **1.** A sealing stopper, usually a cylindro-conical piece of wood, fitted into the mouth of a cask. A safety valve is sometimes used during secondary fermentation to maintain pressure at a maximum of 300 grams per square centimeter. **See also:** spile. **2.** In homebrewing, the rubber or plastic seal into which the fermentation lock is fitted for secondary fermentation in carboys. **3.** A synonym for bung-hole. **4.** British slang for a publican.

bung-hole. The round hole in the bilge of a cask used for filling. **Syn:** bung.

bunging. Sealing a cask with a bung.

bunging apparatus. A safety valve fitted on a storage cask.

bung juice. British slang for beer.

bung stave. Synonym for cant.

burnt sugar. Synonym for caramel.

bürou. Japanese for beer.

Burton ale. **1.** A pale or bitter ale made from gypsum-rich water in the town of Burton-on-Trent in England where beer has been brewed since 1004 and where William Bass opened his first brewery in 1776. **2.** A beer similar in style and taste to those brewed in Burton-on-Trent.

burtonization. The addition of mineral salts to water such as calcium or magnesium sulfate and sodium or calcium chloride.

Burton soda. A cocktail mix of equal parts of ale and ginger beer.

Burton Union System. A system of 24 interconnecting 153-gallon (7 hl) oak casks arranged in two parallel rows in which a yeasty circulatory fermentation takes place. Each cask is fitted with an internal tubular attemperator (heating and cooling tubes) and an external swan-neck pipe at the top. The pipes are connected to a long inclined trough leading to a feeder vessel. During active fermentation, fobbing causes yeast and beer to rise up the pipe and fall into the trough. The yeast tends to sediment and the beer collected in the feeder is returned to the casks through side rods. After 36 hours of fermentation, the wort is transferred to "unions" (four barrel capacity) where it clarifies for five days. The yeast and barm ale works out through the neck, purges itself into a barm back (or yeast trough) and is brought back automatically into the fermenters. This traditional system, unique to Burton-on-Trent, is called "the quiet process." It was shut down by Bass in 1981 and is now used only in the Marston brewery.

Burton water. Hard water from the famous brewing town of Burton-on-Trent in England. An analysis published in an Encyclopedia by Lamirault in 1880 (*Inventaire raisonné des sciences, des lettres et des arts*) gave the following composition in grams per liter: carbonate of lime 0.143, lime sulfate 0.791, magnesium sulfate 0.013, calcium chloride 0.188. **See also:** brewing water.

bush-house. 1. Historically, a temporary ale-house for making beer on the spot such as at a county fair. Etym: So-named because a bush was placed in front of it to mark its location. Also spelled: bushhouse. **2.** Synonym for ale-house.

buska. The name given by early Germans, the Goths, to beer.

butt. A large cask of varying capacity for holding beer, water or wine. In Britain, a butt for beer contains 2 hogsheads or 108 imperial gallons (490.86 liters).

Buttenman. Synonym for Tanzeman.

buttered ale. In old England, an unhopped beverage consisting of sugar, cinnamon, butter and ale.

buttery. Displaying a taste of butter or butterscotch caused by the presence of diacetyl.

button handle. Button- or knob-shaped handle.

butyl acetate. Formula: $CH_3COOC_4H_9$. A butylic ester derived from acetic acid responsible for the fruity odor in beer.

Cc

C. Abbreviation for Centigrade (°C).

Calandra granaria. The scientific name of the grain weevil.

calcium chloride. Formula: $CaCl_2$. A powder, soluble in water and ethanol, used for the treatment of water to make it hard.

calcium disodium EDTA. A foam stabilizing additive used in commercial beers at a rate of about 10 ppm (0.0010%). EDTA stands for ethylenediamine-tetraacetate.

calcium sulfate. Formula: $CaSO_4$. The technical name for gypsum, a mineral salt that imparts hardness to soft water.

Calichal. A drink prepared in Mexico by mixing one part beer and four parts pulque.

cambier. The name given in medieval times to a brewer in the north of France.

Campden tablet. A commercial name for potassium metabisulfite, a source of sulfur dioxide used to prevent oxidation and growth of wild yeasts and bacteria in beer.

Campaign for Real Ale (CAMRA). In Britain, a campaign launched originally by four concerned beer drinkers for the protection and return of non-pasteurized cask-conditioned "Real Ale." Its present membership (1985) numbers more than 17,000 people in 140 local chapters across Great Britain. It was originally called Society for the Preservation of Beers from the Wood later known as the Campaign for the Revitalization of Ale and, in 1973, the present name was adopted. Similar consumer campaigns were launched in The Netherlands (PINT) and in America (Campaign for Better Beer).

Campaign for Better Beer. A campaign launched by the American Homebrewers Association and modeled after the British CAMRA.

CAMRA. Abbreviation for Campaign for Real Ale.

cane sugar. Sucrose obtained from sugarcane.

canette. 1. A German and Swiss drinking mug of tall, conical or cylindrical form popular in the 16th century. **2.** An old French measure for liquids, principally beer.

cann. Now spelled: can. **1.** A drinking vessel shaped like a mug but standing on a molded base and having a single or double scroll handle. **2.** A liquid capacity measure holding one pint.

canned beer. Beer sold in cans. An enameled can suitable for packaging beer was first introduced by the American Can Company in 1934-1935 who tested it with the Gottfried Krueger Brewing Company in Richmond, Virginia. It met with immediate success, and Pabst and Schlitz came out with canned beer the following year.

canning. Transferring fermented beer from the maturation vat to sterilized beer cans.

Canstatter Wasen. An autumn fair held annually in the riverside district of Cannstatt in Stuttgart (Germany). The fair was started in 1818 by the king of Württemberg originally as an agricultural show but it is now the prime rival of the Oktoberfest.

cant. The piece of wood, at the head of a cask, in which a tap hole is pierced. **Syn:** bung-stave.

cap. Short for bottle cap or crown cap.

capper. 1. A general name for instruments used for capping (sealing) beer bottles, usually with crown seals. **Syn:** bottle-capper. **2.** Often refers to a hand tool used with a hammer as opposed to a two-handled capper or hand-lever capper. **See also:** hammer capper.

capping. Synonym for capsuling.

capping machine. An automated machine for capping bottles by pressing and closing crown stoppers around the mouth of the bottle.

capsule. A metallic object of various shapes used to close bottles. **Syn:** seal.

capsuling. The action of closing a bottle with a capsule. **Syn:** capping.

caramel. An amorphous brown mass formed by heating saccharose or dextrose with an acid or alkali. It is used for flavoring and coloring beer. **Syn:** burnt sugar.

caramelized malt. Synonym for caramel malt.

caramel malt. Malt prepared from fully modified sugar-rich barley that is lightly steeped, kiln-dried, re-steeped and heat-dried again at temperatures of 65.5 to 76.7°C (150 to 170°F) for one to two hours, thus converting the soluble starches within the grain into sugar as in mashing. The temperature is then increased to about 120°C (250°F) with frequent check for color. Caramel malt is available in pale (cara-pils) to dark colors and is used in small amounts (12 to 15%) to impart sweetness, aroma and a coppery color to beer. **Syn**: caramelized malt; crystal malt. **See also**: pale crystal malt.

cara-pils. The name given in Europe to pale crystal malt.

carbohydrate. Any of a group of compounds composed of carbon, hydrogen and oxygen (with two atoms of hydrogen for every atom of oxygen) including sugars, starches, and celluloses.

carbonate, to. To inject or dissolve carbon dioxide gas in a liquid such as beer. **See also**: carbonation. **Syn**: to saturate.

carbonation. The process of injecting or dissolving carbon dioxide gas in a liquid to create an effervescence of pleasant taste and texture. In beermaking, one of three methods is used: **1.** injecting the finished beer with the carbon dioxide collected for this purpose during primary fermentation; **2.** kraeusening, or adding young fermenting beer to finished beer to induce a renewed fermentation; **3.** especially in homebrewing, priming (adding sugar) to fermented wort prior to bottling or to each bottle prior to capping to create a secondary fermentation within the bottle. Fermentation in a sealed bottle or container creates carbon dioxide gas which, being trapped, dissolves in the beer. The adjective carbonated usually refers to beers artificially injected with carbon dioxide; when caused by priming, the expression bottle-conditioned is more common. Beers intended to be consumed at low temperatures are usually highly carbonated to compensate for the low temperature and vice versa for beers to be drunk at high temperatures. Bottled beer is always carbonated; U.S. draft beers are usually carbonated, while British draft ales are for the most part cask-conditioned. **Syn**: saturation. **See also**: conditioning.

carbonated. A beer in which carbon dioxide has been injected artificially.

carbonator. An apparatus used in the carbonated beverage industry for introducing carbon dioxide gas into water or sugared water. The efficiency of this apparatus is measured by comparing the quantity of CO_2 injected into a liquid to the amount absorbed by that liquid; this ratio should be as close as possible to 95%. **Syn**: saturator. **See also**: regulator-carbonator.

carbon dioxide. Formula: CO_2. An inert gas responsible for the effervescence in beer. **See also**: carbonation; fermentation.

carbonic acid. 1. Formula: H_2CO_3. A weak and unstable acidic compound formed by the combination of carbon dioxide gas and water. It reacts with bases to form salts called carbonates and bicarbonates and with alcohols and other compounds to form esters such as diethyl carbonate. **2.** In brewing literature this term is often synonymous with carbon dioxide.

carbonyls. A generic name for a group of volatiles which contribute to the flavor of beer. A carbonyl is a radical that is made up of one atom of carbon and one atom of oxygen, connected by a double bond. In beer, the important carbonyls are aldehydes, ketones and oxidation products. These volatiles form by reactions during malting, mashing, fermentation, and aging. Boiling results in a decrease of some volatiles while fermentation increases the concentration of some and decreases that of others.

carboy. A large, narrow-necked glass, plastic or earthenware bottle sometimes encased in wicker or in a plastic or wood frame. Glass carboys, such as those used in homebrewing for secondary or single-stage (blow-by) fermentation, should never be filled with hot wort (98°C, 210°F) because they cannot withstand temperatures above 66°C (150°F).

carmi. In ancient Egypt, diluted zythum. **See also:** zythum.

Carnaval de Binche. A beer festival held annually in Binche, Belgium on Shrove Sunday, Monday and Tuesday. The carnival dates back to the 14th century; gallons of beer are tapped, oranges are thrown and dancing is allowed in the streets.

carrageen. Synonym for Irish moss. **Syn:** carragheen. **See also:** chondrus crispus.

carte. Orthographic variant of quarte.

Cascade. A variety of hops grown in Washington and containing 5.0 to 6.5% alpha acids and 5.0 to 6.0% beta acids.

cask. A barrel-shaped container for holding beer. It was originally made of iron-hooped wooden staves but is now commonly found in stainless steel and aluminum. In England, casks are made in seven sizes: butt (108 gallons, 491 liters), puncheon (72 gal, 327.3 liters), hogshead (54 gal, 246 liters), barrel (36 gal, 164 liters), kilderkin (18 gal, 84 liters), firkin (9 gal, 42 liters), and pin (4 1/2 gal, 21 liters). **Syn:** barrel.

casked ale. **See:** Real Ale.

casked-conditioned. In Britain, ale conditioned in the cask as for Real Ale. Casks of ale are delivered to the pubs where they spend two to three days in cool cellars at a temperature of about 13°C (56°F) while conditioning is completed. **See also:** cellar; cellarman.

casking. The action of racking beer into casks.

cask washer. A machine for washing casks at the brewery.

cask wood. Boards of wood, usually oak, used for making casks. Also spelled: caskwood. **Syn:** stavewood.

cassava beer. Synonym for manioc beer.

catalyst. Any substance that speeds up a chemical reaction, such as in the conversion of starch into sugar, without being changed itself in the process. Enzymes, for example, are natural, organic catalysts.

cation. A positively-charged ion.

caudle. A sort of fortifying soup consisting of wine or ale, eggs, bread, sugar and spices and formerly given to the sick.

celia. Synonym for prima melior.

cellar. 1. Originally, an underground room for storing beer. Now, any thermostatically-controlled room, above or below ground, for storing beer. 2. In English pubs, the cool cellar (12.8 to 18.3°C, 55 to 65°F) where casked ale undergoes further conditioning and maturation before being sold.

cellarage. Storing beer in cool cellars or refrigerated rooms after fermentation for the purpose of conditioning and maturation. By extension, any treatment applied to beer during storage such as fining, racking, filtration, polishing, bottling or blending.

cellarman. 1. At the brewery, the person responsible for the care of beer while it is in the storage room or cellar. 2. In English pubs, the person who receives, stacks and prepares the casks of freshly brewed beer for consumption.

cellulase. An enzyme contained in barley that contributes to the dissolution of the cellulosic protective layer of the granule and allows fermentation to proceed. **Syn:** cytase.

cellulose. Formula: $(C_6H_{10}O_5)_n$. A polysaccharide that forms the structural cell walls of living plants including barley and yeast.

centigrade. Thermometer scale in which the freezing point of water is zero (0°), the boiling point 100°, and the range in between is divided into 100 equal parts. Abbrev: °C. To convert degrees centigrade to degrees Fahrenheit and vice versa:
$$°C = (°F - 32) \times 5/9 \text{ or } (°F - 32) / 1.8$$
$$°F = (°C \times 9/5) + 32 \text{ or } (°C \times 1.8) + 32$$

centiliter. One-hundredth of a liter. Abbrev: cl.

centrifugation. A clarification method using centrifugal force. In brewing, such a force is used to strain and clarify the wort during its cooling stage and the finished beer prior to racking. Essentially, beer is spun is such a way that suspended solids can be removed.

centrifuge. 1. An apparatus generating centrifugal force. 2. A filter using centrifugal force to remove suspended matter.

cereal. Any edible grain of the grass family (*Gramineae*). Includes barley, wheat, oats, maize, millet, rice, rye and sorghum.

cereal adjunct. Synonym for adjunct.

cereal cooker. A vessel in which cereal adjuncts (wheat, rye, oats, rice and maize) are boiled prior to being added to the mash.

cerevisia. The Latin name for a strong beery drink mentioned by Pliny the Elder (23 to 79 AD) in his *Natural History* as the national beverage of the Gauls. The Gallic spelling, *cere visia*, was apparently adapted from Ceres, the goddess of harvest (or cere meaning grain) and vise, meaning strength. In 400 BC the Gauls are said to have prepared cerevisia by boiling barley in a caldron and adding rye, millet, buckwheat, oats or maize, according to what was available. The brew was flavored with herbs and spices such as cumin, coriander, absinth, cinnamon, cockle, or even hops although this has not been clearly established. After primary fermentation the beer was stored in wooden casks (which they invented) until ready to drink. The alcohol content of this beverage is said to have been much higher than that of present-day beer. Julius Caesar prefered cerevisia to wine. The spelling later evolved into cervesia, cervisia, cerudise, cervoise (French), cerveza (Spanish), cerveja (Portuguese), and cervogia (Italian) and formed such words as Saccharomyces cerevisiae. **See also:** cervesia humulina.

cervesariis feliciter. An inscription on a clay goblet dating back to the Gallon-Roman wars. Translated into modern English it would read: "Long live the beer-makers."

cervesia humulina. A hopped-flavored cervesia mentioned in the charter of the Abbey of St. Denis dating back to 768 AD.

cerveza. Spanish for beer.

cervisia mellita. 1. The Latin name for mead, not to be confused with cerevisia, or beer. 2. A type of honey-sweetened beer.

cervoise. An early French name given to non-hopped beer, the equivalent of ale in old England. In the 14th and 15th centuries, when hops were introduced, a distinction was made between cervoise, a nonhopped beer, and bière, which contained hops.

cervoise de miel. The French name for cervisia mellita.

chafer-house. In old England, an alehouse. Etym: Probably from chefer, a saucepan.

chalk. A common name for calcium carbonate, an alkaline salt sometimes used for brewing dark beers.

Champagne du Nord. A sobriquet given by Napoleon's occupying troups to German wheat beer, especially Berliner Weisse.

Champagne mead. A misnomer for sparkling mead.

Champagne of the Spree. A fancy name for Berliner Weisse.

Chancelor ale. A strong ale once brewed at Queen's College, Oxford, on special occasions.

chang. A beer brewed from barley in Nepal and Tibet and drunk in ceremonial vessels.

chaser. A long mild drink, such as beer, taken immediatly after a short strong one to soften its effect.

Chateau collapse-o. British slang for old ale.

cheesy. Possessing a smell or taste of cheese caused by the presence of isovaleric acid caused by the oxidation of isoamyl alcohol.

chemical pathway. A sequence of chemical reactions each of which is catalyzed by an enzyme not supplied by microorganisms. Examples: those that naturally occur in malting and mashing.

cherry beer. See: kriek.

chevalier. In France, a beer glass with a capacity of 2.5 liters.

Chevalier barley. Synonym for two-rowed barley. Etym: Named after the English botanist Rev. J.B. Chevallier who first selected that variety at Debenham, Suffolk, in 1820. Also spelled: Chevallier barley.

chi. A beer brewed from millet by the Lepchas of India.

chicha. The name given to aca, the maize beer of the Incas, by the Spanish Conquistadores. The term was borrowed from the language, Taino, spoken by ancient Hispaniola tribes of Costa Rica, Panama and Colombia, who drank large quantities of this beer. Chicha was made by fermenting maize with or without the addition of fruit juices. In the 19th century chicha was produced commercially: chicha flor, the best quality, was followed by chicha de segunda, the common man's drink prepared by mixing chicha flor with mitaca, (sediments of chicha flor well diluted with water and honey). A third, very poor variety, called runchera, was given to hard laborers and was made by adding more water and honey to chicha de segunda. Also spelled: chichia. **See also:** sora; aca.

chiew. Orthographic variant of chiu.

chill haze. Haziness caused by a combination and precipitation of protein matter and tannin molecules during the secondary process of fermentation. It becomes visible when beer is refrigerated too fast, too cold or too long and soon disappears once the beer warms up. It appears around 0°C (32°F) and disappears around 20°C (68°F). It should not be confused with condensation, which is a film of water forming on the exterior of the glass when the glass and the beer are cold and the ambient air is warm and moist. In homebrewing, proteins can be removed by the addition of polyclar, and tannins can be removed with silica gel. **Syn:** haze. **See also:** chillproofing; colloidal stability.

chilling. The action of cooling the wort after fermentation to cause nitrogenous matter to flocculate and precipitate.

chillproof(ed) beer. A beer treated by one or many chemical substances, usually protein-digesting enzymes, to enable it to withstand low temperatures without clouding. Also known as non-deposit beer or nondeposit beer.

chillproofing. A treatment applied to finished beer to prevent the formation of chill haze when the beer is chilled. Substances are added to provoke one of three reactions: precipitation (as with tannic acid), adsorption (as with bentonite), or hydrolysis (as with proteolytic enzymes). In homebrewing, chillproofing is achieved by adding polyclar and/or silica gel during the second stage of the fermentation process.

chips. Synonym for clarifying chips.

chit, to. To sprout.

chit. The white coleorhiza (or root-sheath) which breaks through the pericarp and testa and protrudes from the base of the barley corn during steeping. These chits constitute the first indication of germination after casting. **See also**: rootlet.

chitting. The appearance of root-sheaths (or rootlets) at the base of the barley corn during steeping.

chiu. A type of wheat beer made in China during the Han dynasty (200 BC, at the beginning of the Chinese Empire) and later. Chiu eventually became the predominant beer style of China and is now a generic word for beer. Also spelled: chiew; kiu. **See also**: shu; t'ien tsiou; pei.

chlorine. Symbol: Cl. An element used in commercial and home brewing in its pure form or as household Javel water as a disinfecting and sterilizing agent. **See also:** javel water.

chocolate malt. Similar to black malt but roasted to a lesser, chocolate-brown color. **Syn:** black malt.

Chondrus crispus. The scientific name for Irish moss, a red seaweed used for clarifying the wort. **See also:** carrageen.

Christmas ale. A special beer brewed in certain countries for yuletide consumption, usually amber-colored or dark-hued, full-bodied, creamy and high in alcohol. Examples include: Aass Jule in Norway, Noche Buena in Mexico, Our Special Ale in San Francisco.

chung. A Tibetan beer made from grim, a type of native barley.

cidery. Having an undesirable taste and smell reminiscent of cider.

citric. Possessing a taste or smell reminiscent of citrus fruits — lemon, lime, orange or grapefruit.

citric acid. Formula: $C_6H_8O_7H_2O$. An organic tricarboxylic acid (containing three carboxyl groups: COOC) occurring in plants, especially citrus fruits, through a complex series of enzymatic reactions known as the Krebs or citric acid cycle.

citric acid cycle. A complex series of enzymatic transformations of elementary sugars (glucose and fructose) that are broken down to acetate (active acetate or acetyl coenzyme A) and the degradation of acetyl results in the transformation of a molecule of citric acid into oxaloacetate. **Syn:** Krebs cycle; tricarboxylic acid circle; TCA cycle.

cl. Abbreviation for centiliter.

clarification. The process of removing suspended particles from the cloudy wort or the finished beer through mechanical (filtration, centrifugation) or chemical means (by adding proteolytic or pectolytic enzymes or flocculating agents (finings)).

clarifier. A long and shallow pan-like fermentation vessel used for certain beermaking processes such as steam beer.

clarifying chips. Thin chips of wood cut so as to present maximum surface with minimum volume or weight and used to assist clarification during secondary fermentation. **Syn:** chips; wood chips; wood strips.

clarifying tub. A large, cylindrical, dome-covered vessel fitted with a false bottom to retain spent grains while allowing the wort to flow. **See also:** decoction mashing.

Clark degree. A unit of water hardness equal to 1 part calcium carbonate to 70,000 parts water; equivalent to 1 grain (0.0648 g) of $CaCO_3$ per imperial gallon of water (10 pounds of water at 62°F or 4.54 kg at 17°C). In England, water is said to be soft when its hardness is less than 5° Clark (70 ppm) and very hard when its hardness is greater than 15° Clark (210 ppm). Etym: Named after T. Clark (1801-1867) who devised a hardness test for water in 1840. Sometimes misspelled: Clarke degree. **Syn:** English degree.

    1° Clark = 14.3 ppm
             = 0.833 grains per United States gallon
             = 143 mg/l calcium ion
             = 0.7 millivals.
             = 0.8 German degree

clean. Devoid of off-flavors.

closed fermentation. A method of anaerobic fermentation in closed containers sometimes under pressure.

cloth filter. A type of filter consisting of cloth stretched between opposing frames.

cloudy. Characteristic of a beer showing turbidity caused by unsettled particulate matter. **Syn:** hazy.

Cluster. A variety of hops cultivated in the United States containing 5.5 to 8.0% alpha acids and 4.5 to 5.5% beta acids.

coarse sludge. Flocculation caused by coagulation of soluble and nonsoluble nitrogenous substances and constituting the first stage of the clarification process of the wort. **See also**: cooler tun.

cock ale. A 17th and 18th century concoction mentioned in American and British cookbooks such as Smith's *Compleat Housewife* (1736). One recipe calls for the following ingredients: 10 imperial gallons (or 12 United States gallons) of ale, 1 large and elderly cock, raisins, mace and cloves.

coeurier. See: Bierkieser.

coirm. An early Irish name for beer.

cold break. 1. The precipitation of protein and tannin material to a fine coagulum during the cooling stage. It starts around 60°C (140°F) and increases as the temperature drops. **Syn**: cold trub. 2. Haziness caused by protein matter which must be strained after the cooling process. **See also**: hot break.

cold lagering. Synonym for lagering.

cold trub. Synonym for cold break.

collar. The layer foam on a glass of beer. **Syn**: head; cream; suds.

colloidal stability. The ability of a beer to resist turbidity or haziness when exposed to cold temperatures. The two main compounds responsible for colloidal stability are the protein fractions and the polyphenolic compounds. **See also**: EBC test.

comb. A utensil to skim away excess foam on a glass of beer.

Comet. A variety of very bitter hops grown in Washington and containing 9.5 to 10.5% alpha acids.

compartment malting. Synonym for box malting.

condenser. In a cooling system, a heat-transfer device that reduces the thermostatic fluid (ammonia, freon 12, freon 22) from a vapor to a liquid state after being in contact with water.

condition, to. To subject beer to conditioning.

condition. The amount of carbon dioxide in a beer.

conditioning. 1. Inducing a secondary fermentation in a closed container for the purpose of creating carbon dioxide gas which, being trapped, dissolves in the beer. Conditioning can be achieved by kraeusening or priming. **See also**: carbonation. 2. Synonym for maturation or aging.

conditioning tank. An airtight tank into which carbon dioxide gas is pumped under high pressure.

congelation. A method for producing stronger beers by freezing the water which can then be removed. **See also**: ice beer; eisbock.

congener. Any of the natural products which form during the fermentation process, including furfurals and aldehydes, and which impart flavor and aroma to beer.

continuous fermentation. A method of fermentation used commercially since 1957. There are two methods presently in use: **1.** the stirred tank method consisting of a cascade system of two or more interconnected stirred fermentation vessels. The yeast is separated by centrifugation and part of it is fed back into the first fermenter. In the first systems of this type the turnover for ale was 16 hours whereas that for lagers was 30 hours. This method is used mostly in New Zealand and in a few breweries in Britain. **2.** the tower method consisting of a cylindrical tower 26 feet high into which wort is pumped through a plug of highly flocculent yeast. In newer methods, such as the Bioreactor systems, fermentation is reduced to two hours. **See also:** batch fermentation.

cooler tun. A flat, open tun placed immediately after the hop strainer and into which the hot wort cools naturally and loses its coarse sludge. **Syn:** coolship.

cooling. The process of lowering the temperature of the boiled wort prior to fermentation. In top fermentation, the wort is cooled down to 14 to 16°C (57.2 to 60.8°F) while in bottom fermentation it must reach 6°C (42.8°F).

coolship. Synonym for cooler tun.

coombs. Synonym for culms.

cooper. **1.** One who makes or repairs wooden barrels and casks. **2.** In England, a drink of equal parts of porter and stout.

cooperage. **1.** The craft of the cooper. **2.** The place where a cooper makes or repairs casks and barrels. **3.** A cooper's fee for his work.

copper. Synonym for brew-kettle.

copus. A drink once made of hot beer, wine and spices.

corn. **1.** In the United States, maize. Corn is often used as a malt adjunct and is cooked to a gelatinized form before being added to the mash. Corn contributes additional starch without adding any particular character or flavor to the beer. Some American brewers use up to 40% corn in their mash. **2.** In Britain, a generic term for certain cereals, especially wheat.

corn cutter. An instrument used by the maltster to cut the barley corn in half and examine its interior. Approximately 50 grains from a harvest are cut to estimate the proportion of grains that have hard and glassy (steely) endosperms as compared to those having the more desirable opaque, mealy appearance. Glassy corns usually have a higher nitrogen content than mealy ones and do not malt as well. Mealy corns on the other hand take up moisture more rapidly than steely ones during steeping. **Syn:** farinator.

corn sugar. Sugar converted from corn starch and refined. **Syn:** glucose; dextrose.

couch. In traditional floor malting, the layer of germinating barley spread on the malt floor after steeping and draining. The first couches are thick (23 to 76 cm) and, after 24 hours or so, the barley is spread more thinly, either by hand or mechanically, to lower the temperature which is then maintained at 15 to 25°C (59 to 77°F) depending on the nature of the malt being produced. In England, prior to 1880, the couch first rested on wooden couch-frames because tax was levied on the volume of steeped grain. Once germination had started, the grain was spread on the malting floor. **See also:** floor malting; piece; matted couche; mat plow; pneumatic malting; radicle; turner.

couching. 1. In traditional floor malting, the action of spreading the steeped barley on the malting floor first in heaps and later, after ploughing, in layers of 10 to 15 centimeters where it germinates. **See also:** floor malting. **2.** In modern pneumatic malting, the procedure of levelling the piece in a compartment to allow the temperature to rise to a specific level, usually around 18 to 21°C (65 to 70°F).

counter pressure. The pressure of air or carbonic gas applied to packaged beer to prevent the escape of carbon dioxide gas, to maintain a constant pressure and guard against the negative effects of oxygen.

courni. An ale-like beverage made by the Britons and Hiberni (or Irish) in the first century BC and mentioned in the works of Dioscorides.

Cranston Bill. See: homebrewing.

crate. A wood, plastic or cardboard box for packing and transporting bottles or cans.

crater. A machine for putting newly filled bottles or cans of beer into crates. **Syn:** recrating machine.

crawler. In Britain, a person who visits every pub in a district and has a drink in each and every one. This activity is known as the "pub crawl."

cream. The froth or foam on beer. **Syn:** head; collar; suds.

cream ale. A blend of top- and bottom-fermented beers, usually more of the second, resulting in a sweet and lightly hop-flavored drink.

creamy. 1. Describes a well-carbonated beer producing a thick, persistent head. **2.** Describes a full-bodied beer possessing a rich, smooth texture.

crop. The yeasts that are skimmed off the surface of top fermenting ale during primary fermentation. **Syn:** outcrop.

crown cap. Synonym for crown cork.

crown-capped. Said of a bottle closed with a crown cork. **Syn:** crown-closed; crown-sealed.

crown-closed. Synonym for crown-capped.

crown cork. A metal cap with a cork or plastic lining and a crown-shaped contour (skirt) which is crimped around the mouth of a bottle to form an airtight seal that retains carbon dioxide gas. The first crown stopper was invented in 1892 by William Painter, founder of the Crown Cork and Seal Company. In 1920 the cork lining was replaced by pressed cork and later by plastic. **Syn**: crown seal; crown cap; crown stopper.

crowner. An automatic machine or hand-tool for pressing crown corks on bottles. A pressure of approximately 250 kilograms per square centimeter is required to press the plastic lining and close the skirt.

crown seal. Synonym for crown cork.

crown-sealed. Synonym for crown-capped.

crown stopper. Synonym for crown cork.

crushing. An operation that mills the malt so as to reduce its interior to a powder form, while leaving the husk intact.

crystal malt. Synonym for caramel malt.

Cubitainer. 1. A commercial name for a one- or five-gallon cube-shaped semi-rigid plastic container used by homebrewers for secondary fermentation. 2. In England, brewers supply take-home draft beer in cubitainers called Polypins.

cuitje. A light beer brewed in Belgium in the 15th century. The double-cuitje, a stronger brew, gave its name to the French expression *double cuite*, splitting headache.

Cullen Act. An amendment to the Volstead Act passed in March 1933 and effective on April 7 of the same year. It authorized the production and sale of beer not exceeding 3.2% alcohol by volume. **Syn**: Cullen-Harrison Act; Beer-Wine Revenue Act.

culms. 1. The name given to rootlets after they have been removed from germinated barley. 2. Synonym for rootlets.

cummins. Synonym for rootlets.

cyser. 1. A variety of melomel prepared by fermenting a must of honey, apple juice and water. 2. Honey-sweetened cider.

cytase. Synonym for cellulase.

cytolysis. The partial disintegration of the cell walls of germinating barley by enzymes. This process begins in the embryo and spreads progressively through the starchy endosperm towards the apex of the grain. Cytolysis reduces the barley's strength rendering it friable and easy to mill. **See also**: modification.

Dd

DAB. Stands for Dortmunder Aktien Brauerei. **See also**: Dortmunder.

dagger ale. An old English expression for strong ale.

dalla. Orthographic variant for talla (q.v.).

Damson-hop alphid. An insect, known scientifically as *Phorodon humuli*, that infects the underside of hop leaves and growing points and eventually, if not destroyed, the cones. **Syn**: hop fly.

Danzig spruce beer. **See**: spruce beer.

dark beer. A general name for dark-colored beers the color of caramelized or roasted malt. The ingredient licorice is partly responsible for the blackish color of some beers, such as porter.

dead mash. Synonym for set mash.

decantation. Drawing off or pouring out without disturbing the sediments.

decanter. A glass bottle with a stopper for holding and serving decanted wine and other beverages.

Deckelpokal. The German name given to a type of covered cup made of metal or glass.

decoction brewing method. Synonym for decoction mashing.

decoction mashing. One of the three brewing methods and one used for bottom-fermenting beers. The process requires three vessels: a mash tun for mash-mixing, a mash kettle (or copper or mash copper) for boiling and a lauter tun (or clarifying tun) for straining. Mashing is carried out in a mash tun, and starts at a low temperature while portions of the mash are taken out and boiled in the mash kettle and later returned to the mash tun thus gradually raising the temperature of the entire mash. The process usually is repeated two or three times and sometimes up to about 13 times and takes five to six hours starting as low as 35°C (95°F) but more often at 45 to 50°C (113 to 122°F) to reach 70 to 76°C (158 to 169°F). The mash is afterwards filtered in a separate vessel known as a lauter tun. **Syn**: decoction brewing method. **See also**: mashing; infusion mashing.

decrating machine. An automatically operated machine to remove empty bottles of beer from crates.

deciliter. One tenth of a liter. Abbrev: dl.

degerminate, to. To remove the rootlets (radicles) from the malted barley after kilning.

degree. In hydrometry, a unit on an arbitrary scale that measures the concentration of solids or alcohol in a solution, equivalent to percent. Equations are available to convert the readings into actual values of specific gravity. The Balling, Baumé, Brix and Plato scales are used to measure the sugar content in aqueous solutions. Sikes degrees, obsolete since 1912, once referred to the alcohol content of a solution. **See also**: Balling; Baumé; Belgian degrees; brewers' pounds; Clark; Plato; Brix; Gay-Lussac; Régie.

degree of modification. In malting, the extent of growth of the acrospire. **See also**: modification.

delabel, to. To remove the label on bottles prior to or during washing.

demi. In France, a beer glass with a capacity, originally, of 1/2 a liter but now more often 33 cl. **See also**: lion; botte; distingué.

demion. An old French liquid measure with a capacity of one quarter of a *pinte*.

demi-posson. An old French capacity measure for liquids equal to one sixty-fourth of a *quarte* or 0.029 liter.

demi-setier. An old French capacity measure for liquids equal to one quarter of a *pinte*.

demistier. An old French wine measure equal to 25.5 cubic inches.

densimeter. An instrument for measuring the density or specific gravity of liquids. It consists, like the hydrometer, of a graduated stem resting on a spindle-shaped float weighted with lead, mercury or pitch. The densimeter is plunged vertically into the liquid and levels off. The density is then read on the graduated stem.

density. The ratio of the mass of a given volume of liquid to that of an equal volume of water at the same temperature.

depitching. Synonym for unpitching.

Depth Charge. A bar drink consisting in immersing a shot-glass full of schnapps into a glass of beer. **See also**: Submarino.

Devil's chapel. The name given to an ale-house in medieval England.

dextrin(e). A complex, unfermentable and tasteless carbohydrate produced by the partial hydrolysis of starch through the action of alpha-amylases during mashing. Dextrins contribute to the final gravity and body of beer; some dextrins remain undissolved in the finished beer giving it a malty sweetness. **See also**: amylase.

dextrinization. The enzymatic process by which alpha amylase degrades soluble starch molecules into dextrin molecules.

dextrin malt. Malted barley with a higher dextrin content and a lower fermentable sugar content than other malts, thus contributing more to the body, sweetness and head retention of beer.

dextrinogenic amylase. Synonym for alpha amylase.

dextrose. Formula: $C_6H_{12}O_6$. 1. A dextrorotatory monosaccharide, member of the class of carbohydrates, occurring naturally in corn and grapes and also found in the blood or formed by the hydrolysis of starch through the action of amylases. 2. The commercial form of refined glucose. **Syn**: corn sugar; grape sugar; glucose.

diacetyl. A volatile compound produced in beer by the oxidative decarboxylation of acetohydroxyl acids (2-acetalactate and 2-acetohydroxybutyrate) produced by yeasts. Diacetyls contribute a butterscotch flavor to beer. **See also**: carbonyls.

diammonium phosphate. An additive used as a yeast nutrient.

diastase. A vegetable amylase enzyme, occurring in the seed of grains and malt, that is capable of changing starches into maltose and later into dextrose. **See also**: amylase.

diastatic. Is said of an enzyme capable of converting starch to sugar. **Syn**: amylolytic.

Diätbier. German for diet beer.

Diest beer. **See**: bière de Diest.

diet beer. 1. Any beer low in sugar or carbohydrates, but not necessarily low in calories ($\pm$ 400 cal/l). In Germany "diet bier" is designed for diabetics and has a relatively high alcoholic content of about 4.75% alcohol by weight or 6.0% by volume. They are called Diätbier in Germany, where the trend originated, and are now produced in other European countries including Britain. **Syn**: diabetic beer. 2. The same term often refers to low-calorie beers brewed for weight-conscious dieters. These beers are not designed for diabetics. **Syn**: light beer.

dimethyl sulfide. **See**: DMS.

dinner ale. Obsolete name for pale ale.

disaccharide. A compound sugar composed of two monosaccharide molecules joined by the elimination of one water molecule.

distiller's beer. Fully fermented, non-hopped, all-malt beer that is distilled directly into whiskey. **Syn**: wash beer.

distinctive. Displaying unique characteristics of flavor and aroma.

distingué. 1. In France, a beer glass with a capacity of 50 centiliters. **See also**: demi; botte; lion. 2. In Belgium, the same word applies to an 80 centiliter size glass.

dizythum. See: zythum.

dl. Abbreviation for deciliter.

DMS. Abbreviation for dimethyl sulfide, a major sulfur compound of lagers not found in British ales because their malts are highly modified at very high temperatures. DMS is released during boiling as a gas that dissipates into the atmosphere. The precursor of DMS, S-methylmethionine, remains present in the wort and converts to DMS if the wort is not cooled rapidly enough (in less than 45 minutes in homebrewing) or if it is allowed to sit after cooling.

Dog's Nose. A mixed drink of hot beer laced with gin and flavored with sugar. **Syn**: Purl.

dolo. A type of millet beer made in Africa. It is brewed locally and varies considerably from one region to another and even within the same region. Neither hopped nor filtered, it is flavored with various bitter plants such as sisal, castor-oil bean, cassia and sometimes pimento and tobacco leaves. Jimson was also an ingredient but was eventually outlawed because of its toxicity. The sugary pulp of cassia is added to increase its alcoholic strength.

domestic brewer. Synonym for homebrewer.

Doppelbock. In Germany, a beer much stronger than simple bock but not necessarily doubly so as the German adjective doppel, meaning double, implies. According to German law, Doppelbock must be brewed from an original wort gravity of 18°P (1.072) to 28°P (1.120) resulting in a strength of 7.5 to 13% alcohol by volume. The brand names of doppel bocks always end with the suffix -ator (Animator, Salvator, Optimator, Delicator, Maximator, Triumphator). The original of the style, named Salvator after the Saviour, was brewed by the Italian monks of the order of St. Francis of Paula, in Bavaria, during the Counter-Revolution period. They were granted permission to sell their product by the court of Bavaria in 1780. The monastic brewery is now operated by the privately owned Paulaner-Thomas-Braü. Also spelled: doppel bock. **See also**: Bockbier; Eisbock.

dopskal. In Sweden, a small drinking bowl with one or two handles, with or without a cover and used, in the 17th century, for serving hot brandy.

dormant. Characteristic of newly harvested barley that exhibits a reluctancy to germinate. **Syn**: immature.

dormancy. The inability of barley grains to germinate immediately after harvesting; varies in intensity between different varieties of barley. Dormancy may last up to a few weeks and ceases during storage when the grains have matured and acquired oxygen. This can be accelerated by steeping the grains in oxygenated solutions. Some types of barleys, especially those grown in cold or maritime climates, grown during a cool, wet season or harvested during a wet spell retain a second type of dormancy called water sensitivity and benefit from steeping to a low moisture content level, with more water being added after an air rest period. **See also**: germinative energy.

Dort. Short for Dortmunder.

Dortmunder. A blond or gold-colored, bottom-fermented beer from Dortmund (Westphalia), Germany's largest brewing city. Although the brewing rights of that city were granted by imperial decree in 1293, the Dortmund style beer was not introduced until the 1840s. The original of this style is often symbolized by the acronym DAB which stands for Dortmunder Aktien Brauerei and is better known locally as Export because it was once brewed for exportation. Outside Germany, in Belgium and Holland, for example, beers brewed in this style are often called Dort. In style it is intermediate between Pilsener and Münchener, darker and less bitter (200 to 220 g/hl of hops as opposed to 400 to 500 g/hl in Pilsener) than the first and drier, less malty (180 to 200 g/hl of hops in münchener) and paler than the second and slightly stronger than both containing 4.2% alcohol by weight or 5.2% by volume. **Syn**: Dort.

double-stage fermentation. Synonym for two-stage fermentation.

dough-in, to. Synonym for to mash.

doughing-in. Mixing ground malt with water, usually 2 to 4 hectoliters per 100 kilograms of malt. **Syn**: mashing-in.

downy mildew. A fungal disease that attacks hops. The fungus, an obligate parasite for hops, overwinters as *mycelium* in the infected rootstock and manifests itself in spring when the buds of the crown start to lengthen. Downy mildew, known scientifically as *Pseudoperonospora humuli*, was first observed in Japan in 1905, in the U.S. in 1909, and was unknown in Britain before 1920.

draff. Synonymous for spent grains.

draft beer. Beer drawn from casks or kegs rather than canned or bottled. Draft beer stored (usually under pressure) in metal kegs is often non-pasteurized and minimally filtered, served from the tap and preferably consumed within one week of brewing (30 days at the limit). **Syn**: tap beer; United Kingdom: draught beer; beer from the wood; beer on tap.

dragon's milk. An old British name for strong ale.

draught. Orthographic variant of draft common in the United Kingdom and the

Commonwealth.

draw, to. To transfer a liquid from one container to another.

drawing off. The action of transferring a liquid from one vessel to another or to bottles and casks.

Dr. Butler's ale. A medicinal ale concocted by the physician of James I, consisting of ale flavored with spices and medicinal herbs.

dregs. The sediments at the bottom of a vessel.

dried malt extract. Synonym for dry malt.

drinking horn. 1. An ancient Greek horn-shaped ceremonial drinking vessel originally made from the horn of an ox or buffalo, or from the ivory of an elephant and later made of earthenware or metal. **2.** Synonym for rhyton.

drinking water. Water suitable for drinking which, by definition, is colorless, odorless, tasteless, devoid of pathogenic or parasite matter, without any chemical pollutants and not over-mineralized. Ideally, potable water should contain, per liter, 125 mg of magnesium, 250 mg of chloride, 250 mg of sulfate, a maximum of 44 mg of nitrates, and 2 g of mineral salts. City water is monitored with regard to bacteriological and chemical purity but mineral salts content varies considerably from one city or region to another. **Syn**: potable water; city water; tap water.

drum malting. A pneumatic malting method using perforated drums fitted with ventilation tubes and rotated along the long axis on supporting rollers.

drum washer. A spraying unit for washing bottles on a revolving drum. The bottles are first soaked in a washing tub after which they are sprayed and jetted while in an upside-down position.

dry. Characteristic of a sugar-free beer as opposed to sweet.

dry hop, to. To added dry hops to fermenting or aging beer to increase its hop character or aroma.

dry hopping. 1. The addition of loose dry hops to the primary fermenter (when the wort has cooled down to 24°C, 75°F), the secondary fermenter or to casked beer to increase the aroma and hop character of the finished beer without affecting its bitterness. Homebrewers usually add 50 to 60 grams of aroma hops or hop pellets per five gallon batch during primary or, more often, secondary fermentation. Hop extracts are not recommended for dry hopping because they contain traces of the organic solvents used for their extraction. **2.** In England, dry hopping more specifically refers to the addition of fresh hops to a cask of draft beer when it is racked from the primary fermenter. **See also**: fermentation hopping.

dry hops. Aromatic (or finishing) hops to be used for dry hopping.

drying. Synonym for kilning.

dry kit. A homebrewing kit consisting of malt flour (or dry malt), hops, malt grains, and sometimes crystal malt.

dry malt. Malt extract in dry, powdered form as opposed to liquid or syrup malt. Dry malt is never hopped. **Syn:** dried malt extract.

dry mead. A mead free of sugar as opposed to sweet mead.

dry priming. In homebrewing, adding corn sugar to the beer before racking to create carbonation.

dry stout. The Irish version of stout, slightly more bitter and higher in alcohol content than the English sweet stout. Dry stout is exemplified by Guinness Extra Stout. **See also:** stout.

Dunder oppe. A mild beer brewed in Brussels in the 15th century.

dunge(on). In early malt kilns, a fire basket located in the lower part of the installation immediately below the kiln floor.

Düsseldorfer Alt(bier). Synonym for Altbier.

dwójniack. A sweet mead produced in Poland by fermenting a must of equal parts of honey and water with an osmophilic yeast. It averages 16% alcohol by volume and is aged for five to seven years in large 4,000 liter wooden vats. Also spelled: dwójniak.

Ee

Early Cluster. A variety of hops grown in Washington containing 7.5 to 8.0% alpha acids.

Easter ale. In old England, a special ale prepared for Easter celebrations.

East Kent Goldings. A variety of hops grown in England containing 9 to 10% alpha acids.

EBC. Acronym for European Brewery Convention. **See also**: EBC test, nephetometer.

EBC test. A test to measure the colloidal stability of beer by storing it at 0°C (32°F) for one night, followed by 48 hours at 60°C (140°F) and another night at 0°C. The turbidity is then measured with a nephelometer in Formazin Turbidity Units (FTU) or EBC Units.

ebulum. In old England, an ale flavored with elder, juniper, ginger and other herbs and spices. Also spelled: ebulam.

effervescence. The bubbling-up or fizz in beer caused by dissolved carbon dioxide gas.

égart. See: Bierkieser

Eighteenth Amendment. See: Prohibition.

Eisbock. The strongest type of bock beers. These ice beers are produced by lagering beer in very cold cellars to the freezing point of water (32°F, well above that of alcohol —173°F) and removing some of the iced water (hence, the name) thereby increasing the alcoholic strength of the beer. Kulminator, the strongest doppelbock in the world (28°P, 13.2% v/v) is produced by this method at the Erste Kulmbacher brewery in Kulmbach near Bayreuth. **Syn**: ice beer. **See also**: Bockbier; congelation; Doppelbock.

EMP pathway. The biochemical sequence of enzymatic reactions (pathway) producing the breakdown of glucose and other carbohydrates. It also is called glucolytic pathway because these reactions are common to both alcohol production and the anaerobic glycosis of muscle. Etym: Named after Embden-Meyerhop-Parnas, three men who conducted research on the mechanism of alcoholic fermentation.

endosperm. The starch-containing sac of the barley grain. The endosperm constitutes 80 to 85% of the dry weight of the grain. Part of this starch serves as a food reserve for the growing embryo during the cytolysis process while the remainder constitutes the bulk of the extract during mashing. The sugars found in the endosperm include glucose, fructose, maltose, sucrose and higher fructosans. Also called: starchy endosperm.

English degree. Synonym for Clark degree.

Entire. The original name for porter.

enzyme. An organic protein substance produced by living cells and which acts as a catalyst in biological and biochemical changes such as synthesis, hydrolysis, oxidative degradation and isomerization. Enzymes are highly specific and act on only one substrate and affect only one reaction or one type of chemical reaction. Alpha-amylase, for example, converts starch to maltotriose and dextrins while beta-amylase converts dextrins to maltose, maltotriose and "a-limit" dextrins. Enzymes are sensitive to heat and undergo denaturation (deactivation) above 50 to 60°C (122 to140°F); they have a low tolerance to a pH of 4.0 or less.

epsomite. Synonym for Epsom salts.

Epsom salts. Formula: $MgSO_4 7H_2O$. Hydrated magnesium sulfate found in solution in mineral waters. Epsom salts are added to brewing water to make it hard. **Syn:** epsomite.

Eroica. A variety of hops grown in Idaho and Washington and containing 10.5 to 11.5% alpha acids.

essential oil. A volatile, odoriferous oily compound found in plants including hops. **See also:** hop oils.

esters. Volatile flavor compounds which form through the interaction of organic acids with alcohols during fermentation and contribute to the fruity aroma and flavor of beer. **See also:** volatiles.

estery. Possessing odors and flavors reminescent of flowers, fruits or vegetables —banana, apple, pear, strawberry and others. **Syn:** fruity.

eswart. See: Bierkieser

ethanol. Synonym for ethyl alcohol.

ethyl alcohol. Formula: C_2H_5OH (or CH_3CH_2OH). A colorless, combustible and potable liquid soluble in water, chloroform, and methyl alcohol. It is the second member of the chemical series of alcohols of the general formula: $C_nH_{2n}OH$. It has a specific gravity of 0.739 at 15.6°C (60°F), a boiling point of 78.3°C (172.9°F) and a calorific energy value of 7 kcal per gram. The term alcohol, when not preceded by a qualification, invariably means ethyl alcohol. Ethanol is the intoxicating element in beer, wine and spirits. **Syn:** alcohol; ethanol; grain alcohol.

ethylaldehyde. Synonym for acetaldehyde.

EtOH. Scientific abbreviation for ethyl alcohol.

European Brewery Convention. An association created in 1947 by a Frenchman named Ph. Kreiss to encourage scientific and technical research. It organizes congresses, conducts collaborative research and develops analytical methods. Acronym: EBC.

exponential phase. Synonym for reproduction phase.

export. 1. Any beer produced for the express purpose of exportation. 2. Generally, the word "export" printed on a label stands for superior quality, a product "suitable for exportation," or a higher than usual alcoholic content. 3. In Germany, a local name for Dortmunder. 4. In Britain, another name for India Pale Ale from the fact that it was once exported to British troops stationed in India. 5. In Belgium, a legal classificaion for strong beers brewed from original wort gravities of 11° to 13.5°P. This classification is now called (since 1974) Catégorie I.

extract. 1. The total amount of dissolved materials in the sweet wort after mashing and lautering malted barley and sometimes malt adjuncts such as corn and rice. Typical composition: 80% carbohydrates (dextrins, fermentable sugars), 8% nitrogenous matter, 5% glycerin, 3 to 4% mineral substances, resins and gums. These extracts in solution determine the starting gravity of the wort, which is expressed in many different ways. It is measured with a saccharometer and expressed in degrees Balling or Plato as the number of grams of extract per 100 grams of wort at 17.5°C (63.5°F). In the United Kingdom it is expressed in brewer's pounds per quarter (336 pounds) of malt (lb/Qr). **See also:** hot-water extract. 2. A concentrate of the essential elements of a substance in a dry or liquid form. **See also:** malt extract.

extract beer. In homebrewer's parlance, beer made from malt extract syrup or powder as opposed to grain beer, which is made from barley (or pre-malted barley).

extraction. The process of removing one element from a complex of others.

Ff

F. Abbreviation for Fahrenheit (°F).

Fahrenheit. A thermometer scale in which the freezing point of water is 32° and the boiling point is 212°. Abbrev: °F. To convert degrees Fahrenheit to degrees Centigrade and vice versa:
$$°F = (°C \times 9/5) + 32 \text{ or } (°C \times 1.8) + 32$$
$$°C = (°F - 32) \times 5/9 \text{ or } (°F - 32) / 1.8$$

FAN. Abbreviation for free amino nitrogen; generally used to characterize the amount of amino acids in the wort. The FAN content is measured and expressed in parts per million (ppm). A wort of 10°B (1.040) contains approximately 220 ppm of FAN, which is ideal for yeast growth. Raw unmalted barley makes an insignificant contribution to the FAN content.

farinator. Synonym for corn cutter.

faro. In Belgium, a blend of equal parts of two types of lambic beer, one of high density (5.5 to 6.0°B) with one of lower density (March beer: lambic of 3.0 to 3.5°B), sweetened with sugar and sometimes colored with caramel and diluted with water. It is now practically extinct and the Vanderlinden de Halle brewery is one of the very last to perpetuate this tradition. Also called: faro-lambic. **See also:** lambic; gueuze; kriek.

faro-lambic. Synonym for faro.

fatty acids. A group of saturated and unsaturated monobasic aliphatic carboxylic acids, all of which impart a foul, soapy flavor to beer, contribute to its staling and affect its head retention.

faucet. Another name for a tap, spigot or stop cock.

ferment, to. To undergo fermentation.

ferment. An enzyme or any substance capable of producing fermentation.

fermentable. Capacity of a solution to undergo fermentation.

fermentation. The chemical conversion of fermentable sugars in the wort into approximately equal parts of ethyl alcohol and carbon dioxide gas, through the action of yeast, resulting in a drop in the specific gravity from an average of 1.045 to about 1.012, but never to 1.000 since unfermented carbohydrates and nitrogen compounds always remain in the beer. There are two basic systems of fermentation in brewing, top fermentation and bottom fermentation, each of which is divided into two basic phases, primary and secondary fermentation. Etym: From the Latin *fervere* meaning to boil. **See also:** top fermentation; bottom fermentation; spontaneous fermentation; hybrid fermentation.

fermenter. A generic name for any open or closed vessel in which primary and secondary fermentation take place. **Syn:** fermentor; fermentation bin; fermentation vessel. **See also:** primary fermenter; secondary fermenter; single-stage fermenter.

fermentation bin. Synonym for fermenter.

fermentation cellar. A thermostatically-controlled storage area, originally a cellar, where fermentation takes place. **Syn:** fermenting cellar.

fermentation hopping. 1. Synonym for dry hopping. 2. In England, a distinction is made between dry hopping, adding hops to ale to be aged in casks, and fermentation hopping, adding dry hops or hop pellets during primary or secondary fermentation.

fermentation lock. In homebrewing, a one-way valve, usually made of glass or plastic, fitted into a centrally pierced cork or rubber bung and attached to the mouth of the carboy or secondary fermenter to allow carbon dioxide gas to escape from the fermenter while excluding ambient wild yeasts, bacteria and contaminants. A fermentation lock is particularly useful for lagers which require long, closed fermentation. It also serves as a guide to the fermentation progress. **Syn:** airlock; bubbler; fermentation valve; water lock; water seal.

fermentation valve. Synonym for fermentation lock.

fermentation vessel. Synonym for fermenter.

fermenting. In the process of fermentation.

fermentor. An orthographic variant for fermenter.

Festbier. In Germany, a special beer brewed for festive occasions, such as Christmas or Easter, or for a local folkloric event or beer festival.

fiery fermentation. Anomalous fermentation characterized by a reduction of froth and the appearance of oily bubbles that burst.

fill, to. The action of filling bottles, cans, casks or kegs.

filler. A machine that pours liquids into bottles and other packaging containers.

filtering. Synonym for filtration.

filter press. A type of filter consisting of cloth-covered frames through which liquids are pumped.

filter pulp. Asbestos or wood pulp pressed into cakes for use in filtration.

filtration. 1. The passage of a liquid through a permeable or porous substance to remove solid matter in suspension. 2. Separating the wort from the spent grains.

final attenuation. Synonym for final degree of attenuation.

final degree of attenuation. The maximum apparent attenuation attainable by a particular wort as determined in a laboratory. The final attenuation depends above all on the proportion of fermentable sugars in the wort, most of which have been transformed before bottling to avoid biological reactions which affect the flavor, head retention and stability of the beer. **Syn:** limit attenuation; final attenuation; attenuation final.

Formula: $A = (B - b)/B \times 100$
A = final degree of attenuation
B = original gravity in °B (or °P)
b = final gravity in °B (or °P).

final gravity. Synonym for final specific gravity.

final S.G. Synonym for final specific gravity.

final specific gravity. The specific gravity of a beer as measured when fermentation is complete (when all fermentable sugars have been converted to alcohol and carbon dioxide gas). **Syn:** final gravity; final S.G.; finishing specific gravity; terminal gravity.

fine, to. To clarify.

fining. A clarifying process that adds organic or mineral settling agents during secondary fermentation to precipitate colloidal matter through coagulation or adsorption. **See also:** finings.

fining agents. Synonym for finings.

finings. Various organic or mineral substances used to ensure a clear beer by causing impurities, yeast cells and other suspended matter to coagulate and precipitate to the bottom of the fermentation container. Isinglass, gelatin, Irish moss, bentonite, white of eggs (or egg albumin), charcoal, wood chips and casein are examples of colloidal agents used for this purpose. **Syn:** fining agents.

finished beer. Technically, fermented and aged beer ready to be racked as opposed to wort or fermenting beer.

finishing hops. Hops added to the wort near the end of the boiling phase or in the fermentation vessel to impart hop aroma and character to the beer as opposed to flavoring hops which contribute to its bitterness. Some brewers recommend adding finishing hops one or two minutes before cooling while others suggest ten or fifteen minutes. Since finishing hops are selected for their aroma rather than for their bittering power, their alpha acid content is usually low. **Syn**: aroma hops; aromatic hops. **See also**: flavoring hops.

finishing specific gravity. Synonym for final specific gravity.

fir(k). Abbreviation for firkin.

fire brewing. A traditional brewing method using direct fire to heat the brew-kettle rather than steam or hot water, thus producing a good rolling boil that apparently improves the fullness and smoothness of beer. In the U.S., Stroh's is one of the few breweries to still use this method.

fire copper. A brew-kettle heated by direct flame.

fire flavor. A roasted or burnt flavor in beer.

firkin. A cask for beer with a capacity of one quarter of a barrel or 9 imperial gallons (40.9 liters). Two firkins equal one kilderkin. Abbrev: fir or firk. **See also**: pin.

first running. Synonym for first wort.

first wort. The first batch of wort to be filtered in the straining vat. It is richer in extract than following batches. **Syn**: original wort; first running. **See also**: second wort.

fish gelatin. Synonym for isinglass.

fish stuffing. In England, a common name for isinglass.

fizz. 1. The effervescence in beer caused by dissolved carbon dioxide gas. 2. A mix of gin and soda, with lemons or limes and ice; usually served in a tall glass.

flagon. 1. Originally, a cylindrical or slightly tapered vessel for sacramental use. It was later adapted to holding or serving wine, water, beer, cider, or other liquors and was then called tankard. 2. A measure of capacity equal to two wine quarts (1.8926 liters).

flaked maize. Partly gelatinized maize, the grain of which has been cracked, moistened, cooked, and flaked between rollers.

flakes. Unmalted adjunct grains in flake form added directly to the mash kettle with the ground malt. Some American brewers use up to 50% flakes in their mash. **See also**: adjunct.

flash pasteurization. A pasteurization method in which the product is held at a higher temperature than in normal pasteurization but for a shorter period of time; draft beer, for example, is steamed to a maximum temperature of 71 to 79°C (160 to 175°F) for 15 to 60 seconds. **See also**: pasteurization.

flat. Is said of a beer lacking in taste because it has little or no effervescence.

flavor. The in-mouth sensations as perceived by the tastebuds. Most of the flavors in beer come from volatiles the composition and concentration of which depend on the raw materials, the type of process (heating, conditioning, maturation), the properties of the yeast strain ,and the development of contaminating microorganisms. **See also**: volatiles; esters.

flavor hops. Synonym for flavoring hops.

flavoring hops. Hops added to the boiling wort to impart bitterness to beer as opposed to finishing hops which contribute to its aroma and hop character. Alpha acids are not soluble in water or wort and only become so when the hops are boiled for at least 60 minutes. The quantity of hops to be added varies according to taste, variety of hops, degree of bitterness desired and brewing method. **Syn**: boiling hops; bittering hops; flavor hops. **See also**: finishing hops.

flavor wheel. A flavor terminology developed by the American Society of Brewing Chemists, the European Brewery Convention and the Master Brewers Association of America in an effort to normalize the description and identification of flavors in beer. A total of 122 terms are divided into 14 classes and represented graphically for easy reference. Copies are obtainable from: American Society of Brewing Chemists, Inc., 3340 Pilot Knob Street, St. Paul, MN 55121, USA.

floating ants. See: p'ei.

flocculate, to. To aggregate into small masses.

flocculating yeast. A bottom fermenting yeast of low attenuation that aggregates into small masses during the break.

flocculation. The phenomenon by which yeast cells aggregate into masses toward the end of the fermentation process. At the break, top- and bottom-fermenting yeast cells can agglomerate and sink to the bottom, thus contributing to the clarification of the beer. The ability of a yeast (either top or bottom) to flocculate or sediment varies with the strain of yeast. **Syn**: breakage. **See also**: non-flocculent yeast; flocculent yeast.

flocculent yeast. A generic name for yeast strains that clump and flocculate during fermentation. **See also**: flocculation.

flooring. Synonym for floor malting.

floor-malting. A traditional germination method that spreads the steeped barley over a flat surface in layers of 10 to 15 centimeters, where it germinates at relatively low temperatures of about 12 to 15°C (52.5 to 59°F), sometimes higher, for up to 13 days. Originally, malting was carried out in winter, autumn or spring to take advantage of the cool weather. Slightly higher temperatures of 14 to 16°C (58 to 62°F) are preferred today. With the introduction of mechanical devices in the 1880s, floor-malting was gradually superseded by pneumatic malting. **Syn**: flooring. **See also**: couch; piece; pneumatic malting.

flowering cone. Synonym for strobile.

fluid ounce. A unit of liquid capacity equal, in the U.S., to 1/16 of a pint or 1.804 cubic inches (29.573 ml) and, in Britain, to 1/20 of a pint or 1.7339 cubic inches (28.412 ml).

foam. The mass of bubbles on a glass of beer. **Syn**: cream; head; froth; collar; suds.

foaming agent. Synonym for heading liquid.

foam retention. Synonym for head retention.

foam stability. Synonym for head retention.

foamy. 1. Covered with foam. 2. Tasting of foam. 3. Said of a beer that generates a good head of foam.

fob. An English brewer's word for froth.

food additive. Synonym for additive.

food-grade. Grade of plastic suitable for containing food. In homebrewing, high density polythene and polypropylene make excellent fermenters. Containers made of lower grade plastic, such as wastebaskets, are inadequate because, for the most part, they impart a "plastic" flavor to the brew.

foot bath. Slang term for a large glass of beer.

Formazin Turbidity Unit. **See**: EBC test; nephelometer.

formidable. 1. In France, a beer glass with a capacity of three liters. **See also**: baron. 2. In Belgium, a beer glass capable of holding one liter.

Forum hordeum. A famous hops market in Hamburg in the 1100s.

fountain. A sort of tap in bars for drawing beer from the cellar to the glass.

four-ale. An obsolete synonym for mild ale.

four-rowed barley. A variety of barley considered as a form for six-rowed barley in which two opposing groups of two rows of grains have been compressed together giving the impression of four rows. This variety is not used in the brewing industry.

framboise. A type of kriek in which the cherries have been replaced by raspberries. **Syn**: frambozenbier. **See also**: lambic; gueuse; kriek.

frambozenbier. Synonym for framboise.

free amino nitrogen. **See**: FAN.

French degree. A French unit of water hardness equal to 1 mg of calcium carbonate ($CaCO_3$) per 1,000 liters of water.

$1°$ French = 10 ppm
= 0.583 grains per U.S. gallon
= 0.7 Clark degrees
= 0.56 German degrees

froth. See: foam; fob; head.

fructose. Formula: $C_6H_{12}O_6$. The sweetest of sugars(173% as sweet as sucrose) found in a natural state in some fruits and in honey or combined with glucose (dextrose) as sucrose.

Frühjahrsbierfest. An annual springtime beer festival held in Munich starting on March 19, St. Joseph's Day.

fruit mead. Synonym for melomel.

fruity. Synonym for estery.

Fuggle. A variety of hops grown in England containing 4.0 to 5.5% and sometimes 6.0% alpha acids and 2.5 to 4.0% beta acids. It is also grown in Oregon with an alpha acid content of 4 to 6%.

full-bodied. Quality of a beer that is rich and mouth-filling as opposed to one that is thin-bodied and watery.

fullness. Synonym for body.

fully modified malt. Malt in which most of the protein materials have been converted by the proteinase enzyme. **See also:** under-modified malt.

fusel alcohols. Synonym for higher alcohols.

Gg

gail. Orthographic variant for gyle.

Galena. A variety of very bitter hops grown in Washington and Idaho and containing 12.5 to 13.5% alpha acids.

gal. Abbreviation for gallon.

galopin. In France, a beer glass of a capacity of 15 centiliters. Because it is so small it is very rare and almost obsolete.

gallon. 1. In the United States , a liquid measure with a capacity of 231 cubic inches (3.7854 liters) equal to 128 fluid ounces. One U.S. gallon = 5/6 of an imperial gallon. Abbrev: U.S. gal. 2. In the U.K. and the Commonwealth, the imperial gallon (or U.K. gallon) is a liquid measure of 277.42 cubic inches (4.5459 liters)(10 lb avoirdupois of water at 17°C), equal to 160 fluid ounces. It is the fundamental unit of capacity in the U.K. and it is defined in the Weights and Measures Act 11/12 Eliz. II of 1963. The gallon is mentioned in Piers Plowman (1342) and it was given legal status as a unit in 1602. The imperial gallon is somewhat larger than the U.S. gallon: 1 imperial gallon = 1.20094 (6/5) U.S. gallons. Abbrev: imp. gal., U.K. gal.

Gambrinus. A corruption or contraction of the name Jean Primus, Duke Jean I of Brabant, Louvain and Antwerp, born in Bourguignon in 1251 and killed in a duel or tournament in Bar in 1295. He is the second patron (not a saint) of brewers and the first patron of beer lovers. He was not a brewer, but a popular ruler well liked by his subjects and particularly by the brewers of Brussels who placed his effigy in the meeting hall of their association in Brussels. According to legend Gambrinus could drink 144 pints of beer during a single feast. His name is synonymous with a joyful and exuberant way of life. Among the other etymological interpretations of the name Gambrinus there is one claiming that it was derived from the founder of Cambray, a brewing city where a brewer was once known as a *gambarius*. Another sees the origin of the word in the medieval German word *gambra* meaning "germination of grain" or from *cambier* the name given to brewers in the North of France in the Middle Ages. Gambrinus is also the name of a Czech brewery established in Plzeň since 1869, a famous café in San Polo di Piave in northern Italy established by a man named Zanotto in 1847 and that of an opera composed by Maurice Frank in 1961.

gassy. Containing excessive carbon dioxide gas.

Gay-Lussac. An alcoholometer devised by Louis Joseph Gay-Lussac (1778-1850) in 1824 to determine the percentage of alcohol in a solution. In France, the alcoholometric strength of a beverage is expressed in terms of its volumetric alcohol content at 15°C (59°F). Pure alcohol has a strength of 100 degrees and the alcohol content is equal to the number of liters of alcohol per 100 liters of wine (or beer). Abrev: °G.L. or °GL.

gel. A colloidal dispersion that does not flow. **See also:** SOL.

gelatin. A colorless, tasteless, and odorless water-soluble protein of little nutritive value prepared from albuminous substances and added to maturing beer to help clarify it.

gelatinization. 1. The imhibition of water and the resulting swelling of starch granules when moist heat is applied to starch. It is the first stage in the enzymatic breakdown of starch followed by liquefaction and saccharification. **2.** The act of cooking malt adjuncts to a gelatinized form prior to adding them to the mash.

German degree. A German unit of water hardness equal to 1 mg of calcium oxide (CaO) per 1,000 liters of water.
$$1° \text{ German} = 17.9 \text{ ppm of } CaCO_3$$
$$= 1.4285 \text{ Clark degrees}$$
$$= 1.044 \text{ grains per US gallon}$$
$$= 1.78 \text{ French degrees.}$$

germinal brush. Synonym for grain brush.

germinating. Synonym for germination.

germination. The second stage of the beer making process that drains the steeped barley grains and allows them to sprout for seven to nine days. The process may be accelerated by the use of such products as gibberellic acid or may be prolonged up to 11 or 13 days for a more thorough disintegration of the malt. While germinating, the embryo produces the enzyme amylase (sometimes called diastase), which will later convert some of the starch of the endosperm into maltose and dextrins. This treatment of the barley grains follows cleaning, sorting, grading and steeping and takes place at 10 to 20°C (50 to 68°F). **See also:** malting; floor malting; germination box.

germination box. A large, rectangular, open-topped container with a capacity of about 200 quarters, often made of cement, fitted with a removable slotted bottom plate located about 20 centimeters from the bottom and through which air of appropriate temperature and humidity is allowed to circulate. The barley grains, in layers of 60 to 100 centimeters, are constantly turned by a five-bladed propeller fitted on a vertical shaft. The process takes about six days. Also called: Saladin box.

germinative capacity. The percentage number of barley grains to have germinated in laboratory tests after six days in moist sand or damp filter pads. **See also:** germinative energy; Thunaeus test.

germinative energy. The percentage of barley grains to germinate under specific conditions. In laboratory tests, one hundred or a few hundred barley grains are germinated in moist sand or between damp filter pads on petri-dishes (9 mm) at 15 to 20°C (50 to 68°F). After three days the number of corns that have chitted are counted and that value constitutes the germinative energy, which should be over 95% and preferably closer to 98%. At least three sets of 100 grains each are used in each test. A second count, taken after six days, constitutes the germinative capacity. The difference between the germinative capacity and the germinative energy is a measure of the dormancy of the barley grain.

germinative power. The capacity of barley grains to germinate; it must be over 98% to be acceptable for malting.

gibberellic acid. Formula: essentially Ga_3. A microbiological product having plant growth hormones extracted from a parasite mushroom (the fungus *Gibberella fujikuroi*) from Japanese rice fields and identical to a material secreted by the barley embryo. It is added to steeping water at a rate of 0.5 mg per kg of barley to break dormancy and to accelerate plant growth. Also, it is sprayed on germinating barley at about 0.25 mg/kg to trigger or accelerate germination, hasten the secretion and action of proteolytic enzymes, the respiration rate, the modification rate, the heat production rate, and the growth of the embryo, thus reducing germination time. On the other hand, it has very little effect on amylase.

Gildenbier. A Belgian word meaning corporation beer (bière de corporation), synonymous with bière de Diest.

gill. 1. A capacity measure for liquids equal to one quarter of a pint. It first came into use in the 13th century as a wine measure. 2. Ground ivy (a flower of the genus Nepeta of the Laviatae family) or beer flavored with it instead of hops.

ginger ale. A non-alcoholic, carbonated beverage flavored with ginger. **Syn:** ginger beer.

Ginger Beer. 1. A cocktail consisting of one part Champagne, one part framboise, one part ginger ale, three parts beer, and a touch of powdered ginger. 2. A fermented beverage of syrup of ginger.

GL. Abbreviation for Gay-Lussac. Also: G.L.

glass. 1. A drinking vessel made of glass. 2. The contents of such a vessel, when referred to in terms of its quantity.

glucoamylase. Synonym for amyloglucosidase.

glucose. A simple fermentable sugar formed in the wort by the enzymatic action of yeast on maltose and maltotriose. In industry it is obtained by the hydrolysis of starch with dilute acids. Pure, commercial glucose, sometimes called dextrose, always contains a certain amount of dextrins which, being unfermentable, remain in the beer and give it a sweet, mellow flavor. **Syn**: dextrose; corn sugar.

glume. Either of the empty sterile bracts at the base of a grass spikelet, or a similar structure on the spikelets of sedges.

goblet. 1. A drinking vessel similar to a chalice, with a deep bowl on a proportionately short stem, without a handle, and which has a capacity, in English glassware, of one gill or more. 2. In modern stemware classification, the goblet is the tallest glass and holds 9 to 12 fluid ounces.

godisgood. An early name given to yeast by English brewers who did not understand its chemistry and workings but guessed that it was responsible for fermentation. Also spelled: godesgood; goddisgood.

Goldings. A variety of hops grown in England and containing 4.6 to 5.2% alpha acids.

gondale. The name given in medieval France to a type of beer brewed in the city of Lille. The term is derived from goodale and goodall.

goods. A brewer's term for the total content of the mash tun at the end of the mashing process.

goudalier. The name given in medieval times to a beer merchant in the north of France.

goût de jeune. The French name given to the unpleasant smell associated with green beer. In German: Jungbukett. **See also**: green beer.

grading. The process of sorting barley grains according to size.

grain alcohol. Synonym for ethyl alcohol.

grain beer. Beer made from malted barley rather than from malt extract. **Syn**: all-grain beer.

grain brush. In malting, a machine used mainly at the end of the cleaning process to remove impurities adhering to the surface of barley grains. **Syn**: germinal brush.

grains of paradise. The seeds of a spice, *Amomum melegueta*, grown in West Africa and once used to flavor ale and later gin and cordials.

grain weevil. An insect, known scientifically as *Calandra granaria*, that feeds on and infects the malt. **Syn**: malt worm.

granny. In Britain, a mix of old and mild ale.

grant. A small cylindrical vessel, usually made of copper, fitted with one or more drain cocks for draining and inspecting the mash when it is transferred from the mash tub to the lauter tub.

grave ale. A Danish tradition in which friends share a feast at or after a funeral to "keep away" the spirit of the departed. The beer served on this occasion was named grave ale.

green beer. Newly fermented beer before maturing or lagering. At this stage one of two products can be obtained: scotch or beer. Scotch is produced by distilling fermented, unhopped wort. **See also:** goût de jeune.

green malt. Newly germinated barley not yet dried or kilned.

grinder. A machine generally consisting of two or four pairs of cylinders (or rollers) through which malted barley is crushed two or three times. **Syn:** malt mill; malt crusher; mill; roller mill.

grinding. Synonym for milling.

gripperhead. The part of an automatic filling machine that grips the head (or neck) of the bottle.

grist. 1. Grains to be ground. 2. Sieved and ground malt ready for mashing. 3. A quantity of ground malt sufficient for one mashing.

grist cage. A large conical-shaped vessel into which grist is collected after milling.

grit. Adjuncts, e.g. cereal grains used as substitutes for barley. **Syn:** raw grain.

grouchevoï. Kvas in which pears have macerated. **See also:** perry.

growler. A jug-like or pail-like container once used to carry draft beer bought by the measure at the local tavern.

gruit. A mixture of herbs and spices, principally sweet gale or bog-myrtle and marsh or wild rosemary, coriander, yarrow, milfoil and other ingredients such as juniper berries, caraway seed, aniseed, ginger, nutmeg and cinnamon once used to flavor English and European ales before the introduction of hops. Hops and sometimes resin also entered in the composition of gruit in some countries. After the creation of the first brewers corporation, the preparation of gruit became the work of specialists who operated in gruthouses or gruit houses. Once spelled: grut; gruyt; grug; gruz.

gruitbier. From the Middle Ages to the 15th century, a beer flavored with gruit. **See also:** gruit.

gueuze. In Belgium, a beer prepared by blending two lambic beers of different age, a young lambic with an old one, usually in a ratio of two to one. This blending causes a new fermentation to occur and the brew is bottled and aged for one more year producing a dry, fruity beer with Champagne-like effervescence. It contains about 4.4% alcohol by weight or 5.5% by volume (5.2° Belgian). Etym: From the name of a street in Belgium, Guezenstraet (rue des Gueux), where this type of beer was once sold. Gueux means beggar or vagabond. Also, it is claimed to have been introduced in 1870 by the brewer and burgomaster of Lembecq who hired the engineer Cayerts to apply the technique of bottle-conditioning as practiced in Champagne to the production of lambic. The product was first called "lambic de chez le gueux" and later, "lambic du gueux." Also spelled in English: geuze. **Syn**: gueuze-lambic. **See also**: cherry beer; lambic; faro; framboise; kriek; Mort Subite.

gueuze-lambic. Synonym for gueuze.

gumming. The action of spraying a coat of glue on beer labels.

gushing beer. A beer which foams out vigorously when uncapped. **Syn**: wild beer.

gyle. 1. The portion of unfermented wort added to finished beer to condition it and raise its alcohol content. **2**.The quantity of beer produced by a single brewing. Sometimes spelled: gail. **3**. A fermentation vessel.

gyle vat. In old English, a fermentation vessel.

gyngleboy. In 16-th century England, a leather bottle or black jack lined with silver or gilt metal and ornamented with silver bells which, according to Thomas Dekker (*The Seven Deadly Sins of London*, 1606), rang "pearles of drunkeness."

gypsum. Formula: $CaSO_42H_2O$. Hydrated calcium sulfate used in the treatment of soft or neutral water to harden it. **Syn**: plaster of Paris.

Hh

Hag. A type of beer produced in ancient Egypt (ca 2000 BC) from what was called "red barley of the Nile." Also spelled: hek; hequ(p) hak.

haircloth. A horsehair blanket placed on the floor of traditional hop-drying kilns. **Syn**: horse-hair cloth.

Halbe. In Germany, a beer mug with a capacity of half a liter. **See also:** Masskrug.

Half-and-Half. A blend of equal parts of drinks of the same nature such as mild and bitter, ale and stout or ale and porter.

Hallertau. A variety of hops cultivated in Bavarian Germany containing 7.0 to 8.0% alpha acids. Because of disease, it is being replaced by Brewer's gold, Northern Brewer and Hersbrucker. The same variety, grown in Washington and Idaho, yields 5.0 to 6.5% alpha acids and 4.0 to 6.0% beta acids. Depending upon usage, Hallertauer is used.

hammer capper. A manual bottle capper used with a hammer.

harbor beer. Slang expression for very weak beer.

hardness (of water). Synonym for water hardness; the quality of water in relation to the amount of calcium and magnesium salts it contains.

hard resins. During their storage, alpha and beta acids gradually oxidize and polymerize and lose their crystalline structure, their aroma and their bittering and preservative powers to become amorphous bodies. In the later stages of this conversion hard resins are formed that are useless in the brewing process. The process is called resinification. **See also:** soft resins.

hard water. Water containing larger than usual quantities of calcium and magnesium salts.

harsh. Synonym for astringent.

haze. Abbreviated form of chill haze.

hazy. Synonym for cloudy.

HBU. 1. Abbreviation for hop bitterness unit. 2. Abbreviation for homebrewers bittering unit.

head. 1. The foam at the top of a glass of beer. **Syn**: cream; collar; foam; suds. 2. The froth that forms on top of the wort during primary fermentation. 3. The flat end of a cask or barrel.

head brewer. Synonym for master-brewer.

heading liquid. An additive used to ensure a firm, long-lasting head or to increase its thickness. **Syn**: foaming agent; heading compound.

head retention. The foam stability of a beer as measured, in seconds, by the time required for a 3-centimeter foam collar to collapse. **Syn**: foam stability; foam retention.

headspace. Synonym for ullage.

heat chamber. The part of the kiln where heat is stored and distributed evenly under the floor of the kiln.

Heater and Cooler. A short glass of liquor followed by a tall glass of beer.

heat exchanger. Process equipment for heating or cooling the wort or beer rapidly.

heavy beer. Synonym for high gravity beer.

heavy wet. An old name for strong ale.

hectoliter. One hundred liters. About 22 (21.9976) imperial gallons or 26.4 United States gallons. Abbrev: hl.

herb beer. A misnomer for fermented sugar flavored with herbs. **Syn**: herb wine.

Hersbrucker. A variety of hops grown in Washington and containing 5.0 to 6.5% alpha acids, sometimes less.

hexose. Any monosaccharide containing six carbon atoms; includes glucose, fructose, lactose, mannose, galactose.

Het Pint. A traditional Scottish drink consisting of ale, whiskey and eggs.

higher alcohols. Alcohols of higher boiling point than ethanol, which are derived from keto-acids during the yeast protein synthesis. The formation of higher alcohols varies with yeast strain and yeast growth, fermentation temperature (an increase in temperature is followed by an increase in the formation of alcohols), and fermentation method (in some cases a stirred fermentation produces more alcohols). There are two classes of higher (fusel) alcohols. Volatile alcohols, most often called aliphatic alcohols, form one class (examples: propyl alcohols, butyl alcohol, amyl alcohols). The other class is non-volatile alcohols (examples: phenol alcohols like tyrosal). **Syn:** alcohols; fusel alcohols. **See also:** volatiles.

high fermentation. Synonym for top fermentation.

hhd. Abbreviation for hogshead.

hiya. In Japan, cold saké.

high gravity beer. Any beer brewed from an original wort gravity of 1.047 or more. **Syn:** heavy beer.

high kraeusen. See: kraeusen.

hippocras. A combination of melomel and metheglin, a mead of honey, raisin juice and herbs and spices once prepared for medicinal purposes. Etym: Named after Hippocrates (460-377 BC), Greek writer and Father of medicine.

hl. Abbreviation for hectoliter.

hoan tsie'u. A type of Chinese saké. The term means yellow rice wine.

Hoegaardse Wit. Synonym for blanche de Hoegaarden.

hogs. Abbreviation for hogshead.

hogshead. 1. A large barrel-shaped cask for holding liquids, the capacity of which ranges from 54 to 140 gallons. 2. A precise capacity measure that once varied according to the liquid or commodity it contained, originally equal to 63 old wine gallons (52.5 imperial gallons). The London hogshead for beer had a volume of 54 gallons while that for ale had a volume of 48 gallons. Today, it has a volume of 63 gallons (238.5 liters) in the USA and 54 imperial gallons (245 liters) in the U.K. Abbrev: hhd or hogs.

homebrew. A beer made at home. **Syn:** homemade beer; homebrewed beer.

homebrewer. One who brews beer for personal consumption. **Syn:** amateur brewer; domestic brewer.

homebrewing. The art of making beer at home. In the United States, home-brewing was legalized by President Carter on February 1, 1979, by an act of Congress introduced by Alan Cranston. The Cranston Bill allows a single person to brew up to 100 gallons of beer annually for personal enjoyment and up to 200 gallons in a household of two persons or more aged 18 and older. In England, homebrewing was again legalized in 1963 by Chancellor Reginald Maudling who lifted all restrictions on homebrewing, provided it was not sold.

homebrewers bittering units. A formula devised by the American Home-brewers Association to estimate the bitterness value of hopped malt extract by multiplying the equivalent number of ounces of hops by the alpha acid percent of the hops employed. Example: If 2 ounces of 5% alpha acid hops are present in a 3.3 pound can of hopped malt extract this would yield a 10.0 HBU per 3.3 pounds. Abbrev: HBU. **See also**: alpha acid units; bitterness units; hop bittering coefficient; hop bitterness units; bittering units.

Honeybeer. A cocktail prepared by heating a pint of ale and adding one soupspoon of honey.

honey wine. 1. A synonym for mead. The term is rejected by many wine purists and legislators (including those of France) who maintain that the term wine can only apply to a product of the vine. 2. Synonym for pyment.

hoop. The circular band of metal surrounding the staves of a wooden cask or barrel and holding them together.

hoop binding. 1. The action of binding together the staves of a wooden barrel or cask. 2. The circular piece of metal used for that purpose.

hop, to. To add hops to the wort or the fermenting beer.

hop back. A large sieving vessel fitted with a perforated false bottom to separate the spent hops from the bitter wort after boiling. **Syn**: strainer; hop jack; hop strainer. **See also**: Moor's head; hop separator.

hop bine. The growing stem of the hop plant. **Syn**: bine.

hop bittering coefficient. The coefficient obtained when multiplying the alpha acid percentage of a variety of hops by the number of ounces to be boiled in the wort. This coefficient is useful to homebrewers when the hop variety mentioned in a recipe is not available and another must be substituted. For example, 2 ounces of hops at 5.25% alpha acids can be substituted in a recipe calling for 1.5 ounces of hops at 7% alpha acids. **See also**: alpha acid units; hop bitterness units; bitterness units; bittering units; homebrewers bittering units.

hop bitterness units. A formula devised by F. Eckhardt to calculate the bitterness of a homebrewed beer or the amount of hops required to produce a beer of a predetermined bitterness level.

Formula: $HBU = (a \times w)/K$

a = alpha acid percentage of hops: whole, pellets or extract.

w = a constant based on weight of hops divided by volume of beer:
ounces per gallons: oz/U.S. gal — oz/U.K. gal
grams per gallon: g/U.S. gal — g/U.K. gal
grams per liter: g/l.
Example: 1.5 oz of hops per 5 U.S. gal batch = 0.3 oz/U.S. gal.

K = a constant based on figures obtained from technical sources. It varies according to the system of units used for "w":
= 0.093 for oz/U.S. gal
= 0.078 for oz/U.K. gal
= 2.7 for g/U.S. gal
= 3.2 for g/U.K. gal
= 0.7 for g/l

Conversely, the amount of hops to be used to obtain a determined bitterness unit can be calculated by rearranging the formula:

$$w = K / (a / HBU)$$

Abbrev: HBU. **See also**: alpha acid units; bitterness units; bittering units; homebrewers bittering units; hop bittering coefficient.

hop break. The precipitation of protein and tannic material when hops are added to the boiling wort. A new hop or hot break occurs with each addition of hops.

hop cone. Synonym for strobile.

hop essential oils. Synonym for hop oils.

hop extract. Bitter resins and hop oils extracted from hops by organic solvents, usually methylene chloride or hexane, while tannins, sugars, and proteins are extracted with hot water. The solvents and water are later removed by evaporation. The use of such extracts is increasing in the brewing industry because they store well, they are less bulky, they require no refrigeration, boiling time is shorter and straining spent hops is not required. Hop extracts are sometimes isomerized by alkalis or by magnesium salts at neutrality, or by exposure to light of specific wavelength. Iso-alpha-acid hop extract (or isomerized hop extract) is added as late as possible usually during secondary fermentation.

hop field. Synonym for hop garden.

hop flea beetle. An insect, known scientifically as *Psylloides attenuata*, that eats holes in young hop leaves.

hop flour. Obsolete synonym for lupulin.

hop flower. Synonym for strobile.

hop fly. Synonym for Damson-hop alphid.

hop garden. A field where hops are cultivated. **Syn**: hop field.

hop grower. One who grows hops.

hop jack. Synonym for hop back.

hop kiln. An oast house in which hops are dried 24 hours after picking at 75 to 80°C (167 to 176°F) to 8 to10% moisture.

hopping. The addition of hops to the boiling wort or fermenting beer. **See also**: dry hopping; fermentation hopping; boiler hopping; late hopping; alpha acid; beta acid; hop oils.

hopping beer. An early name given in England to hopped beer as opposed to unhopped "spiced ale."

hop mill. Synonym for hop tearing machine.

hop mold. A disease produced by the fungus *Sphaerotheca macularis* that attacks hops. **Syn**: white mold; red mold; powdery mildew.

hop oils. 1. One of the two fractions of lupulin (the other being soft resins). Hop oils belong to the terpene group of hydrocarbons and contain several hundred different compounds of which terpene hydrocarbons account for about 70%, alcohols (mainly geraniol and linalool) constitute the remaining 30%. Other constituents include aldehyde and esters. Hop oils are responsible for the hop aroma or character of beer. Like all essential oils, they are very volatile and are largely lost by steam evaporation during the boil. **Syn**: hop essential oils. **See also**: soft resins. 2. A concentrated oil extracted from hops.

hop pellets. Highly processed hops consisting of finely powdered hop cones compressed into pea-size tablets used in both home and commercial brewing. Regular hop pellets are, by weight, 20 to 30% stronger than the same variety in loose form; one pound of hop cones yields about 10 to 12 ounces of pellets. Concentrated pellets, as used in the brewing industry, are first processed to remove the non-resinous material, thus reducing the weight and volume. Standardized pellets are made from blends of hops to obtain a specific alpha acid level. Hop pellets keep better when stored in a sealed container around 12°C (54°F). **Syn**: pelletized hops.

hop rate. The quantity of hops to be added to a given volume of sweet wort during boiling. In commercial brewing, hop rates are quoted in pounds per barrel or grams per hectoliter while homebrewers refer to ounces per five gallons.

hop resin. Highly processed hops consisting of hop resins and oils extracted by solvent.

hop(s). A perennial climbing vine, also known by the Latin botanical name of *Humulus lupulus*, a member of the natural family of *Cannabinaceae*; hence, a close relative of *Cannabis sativa*. The female plant yields flowers of soft-leaved pine-like cones (called strobile) measuring about an inch in length. Only the female ripened flower is used for flavoring beer. Because hops reproduce through cuttings, the male plant is not cultivated and is even routed-out to prevent them from fertilizing the female plant, the cones of which would then become weighed-down with seeds. Seedless hops have a much higher bittering power than seeded ones. There are presently over one hundred varieties of hops cultivated around the world. The best known are: Brewer's Gold, Bullion, Cascade, Cluster, Comet, Eroica, Fuggles, Galena, Goldings, Hallertauer, Nugget, Northern Brewer, Perle, Saaz, Styrian Goldings, Tettnanger, Willamettes, Wye Target. Hops are grown in Czechoslovakia, Bavaria (W. Germany), Kent (England), Tasmania (Australia) and Yakima Valley (Washington). Apart from contributing bitterness, hops impart aroma and flavor, reduce the surface tension during the boiling stage, assist in forming a yeast head during ale fermentation and inhibit the growth of bacteria in wort and beer. Hops are added at the beginning of the boiling stage (called flavoring, boiling or bittering hops) to give the brew its bitter flavor and at the end of the boil (called finishing or aromatic hops) to give it aroma and hop character. In commercial brewing, about 200 to 700 grams of hops are required for every hectoliter of wort. The addition of hops to beer dates from between the 10th and the 7th century BC; however, hops were used to flavor beer in pharaonic Egypt at least 600 years BC. They were cultivated in Germany as early as the 3rd century AD and were used extensively in French and German monasteries in medieval times and gradually superseded other herbs and spices around the 14th and 15th centuries. Pépin le Bref, ruler of the Franks, gave hop gardens (called humlonaria) to the Abbey of St. Denis, near Paris, in 768. Hop fields also were cultivated at the Abbey of St. Germain des Prés in 800 and at the Abbey of Corvey sur le Wesser in 822. In Flanders, Jean Sans Peur founded the *Ordre du Houblon* in 1409 to encourage the use of hops in beermaking. Prior to the use of hops, beer was flavored with herbs and spices such as juniper, coriander, romarin, cumin, nutmeg, oak leaves, lime blossoms, cloves, rosemary, gentian, guassia, camomille and others. **See also**: hop oils; soft resins; lupulin; Humulus lupulus; kiln-dried hops; alpha acid; beta acid; preservative value.

hop separator. A chest-like vessel containing a sieve and a screw conveyor for removing spent hops and for squeezing the wort out of them. It is used in some breweries instead of the hop back.

hop strainer. Synonym for hop back.

hop tannin. Tannins derived from hops as opposed to malt tannins. **See also**: tannin.

hop tearing machine. An apparatus that separates the various parts of the hops: lupulin, bracts, stems. **Syn**: hop mill.

hop tonic. A non-alcoholic beer once brewed at home as a temperance beverage but suspected of often containing various amounts of alcohol.

hoppy. Displaying the characteristic odor of hops.

hordein. A protein (prolamine) found in barley.

Hordeum distichum. The botanical name for two-rowed barley.

Hordeum hexastichum. The botanical name for six-rowed barley.

Hordeum spontaneum. A wild grass believed to be the principal ancestor of barley.

horse-hair cloth. Synonym for haircloth.

hose, to. To draw beer from the fermentation vessel to the storage cellar.

hosing. Drawing beer from the fermentation vessel to the storage cellar.

hospitality room. A special room in a brewery where visiting guests are invited to taste the products of the brewery.

hot break. 1. The coagulation and precipitation of protein matter during the boiling stage. In homebrewing, hot break trub can be improved by the addition of Irish moss during the last fifteen minutes of the boil or it can be removed with a hop-back filtration of the wort or by allowing the hot wort to settle out before drawing it to the wort chiller. **Syn:** hot break trub; hot trub. **See also:** cold break; hop break. **2.** Haziness caused by protein sediments.

hot-break trub. Synonym for hot break.

hot trub. Synonym for hot break.

hot-water extract. In laboratory tests, the quantity of dissolved solids present in a sweet wort solution prepared from malt and/or other materials. Abbrev.: HWE.

household sugar. A common name for cane sugar or sucrose.

Huckle-my-buff. In England, a mix of hot beer, brandy and eggs.

humlonaria. The name given to hop yards or gardens given to the Abbey of St. Denis by King Pépin le Bref in 768. Hop yards are also mentioned as *humularium* in the records of the Bishopric of Freising in Upper Bavaria between 855 and 875.

humulon(e). Synonym for alpha acid, one of the two resins found in hops, composed of humulone, cohumulone and adhumulone.

Humulus lupulus. The Latin botanical name for hops. The Romans called it *Lupus salictarius* because the plant grew wild among the willows like a wolf.

hukster. In medieval England, a woman who retailed beer and ale, which she bought from the brewster or ale-wife.

husar(d). Synonym for husky grain.

husk. The dry outer layer of certain cereal seeds. The husk of barley consists of two closely adherent straw-like bracts (the lemma and the palea) which partially overlap. The barley husk provides protection for the grain, endosperm and growing acrospire during the various stages of the malting process. It also plays an important role as a filter-bed during lautering.

husky grain. Overgrown malt the acrospire of which reaches beyond the end of the grain. **Syn:** husar(d); overgrown malt.

HWE. Abbreviation for hot-water extract.

hydrogen-ion concentration. The concentration of hydrogen ions in a solution, usually expressed in pH units, and used as a measure of the normality of the solution. **See also:** pH.

hydrolysis. The degradation or alteration of an organic substance by water. The molecular composition of both the substance and the water are split and the ions of water, OH (hydroxyl) and H (hydrogen) each react with a fraction of the cleaved substance. The presence of an acid or alkali is usually needed to act as catalyst. For example, proteins are hydrolyzed to amino acids, alcohol plus acid form esters, and disaccharides yield monosaccharides. Example, sucrose hydrolyzes into glucose and fructose.
   Formula: $C_{12}H_{22}O_{11} = C_6H_{12}O_5 + C_6H_{12}O_6$.

hydromel. 1. The French word for mead. **2.** In English, a weak or diluted mead.

hydrometer. A glass instrument for measuring the specific gravity of liquids as compared to that of water, consisting of a graduated stem resting on a weighed float. Most hydrometers are calibrated for use at 15.6°C (60°F) and tables or charts are provided listing corrections for variations to that temperature. The accuracy of a hydrometer is tested in water at 15.6°C (60°F) where it should read zero. **See also:** hydrometer jar.

hydrometer float. The bulb- or spindle-shaped float of a hydrometer weighed with lead, mercury or pitch.

hydrometer jar. A tall, cylindrical, transparent glass or plastic jar in which the liquid to be measured is poured. The hydrometer is then floated in the liquid and spinned to dislodge adhering bubbles. The reading is taken at the waterline. **Syn:** testing jar; test tube.

iablochny. Kvas in which apples have macerated.

I.B.U. Abbreviation for International Bitterness Unit. Also written: IBU.

ice beer. **See:** Eisbock.

imiak. Name given in Greenland to a home-brewed malt beer.

immature. Synonym for dormant.

immersion heater. A thermostatically-controlled heating device, usually 50 watts strong, used by home brewers for maintaining a constant temperature in the mash tun.

imperial gallon. A capacity measure in the United Kingdom and the Commonwealth equivalent to 1.2 United States gallons or 4 liters. **Syn**: U.K. gallon. **See also**: gallon.

imperial pint. **See:** pint.

imperial quart. A liquid measure of the United Kingdom and the Commonwealth with a capacity of one quarter of a gallon, 40 fluid ounces or 69.318 cubic inches (1.135 liters).

Imperial Russian stout. Synonym for Russian stout.

Imperial stout. Synonym for Russian stout.

Indian corn. A popular name for maize.

India pale ale. 1. An ale brewed in England for British troops stationed in India in the 18th century. It was brewed very strong to survive a voyage that could take as much as six months. The term now refers to bottled pale ales, specially those intended for exportation. **2.** Trade name for a beer brewed by Labatt in Canada and known as IPA.

indirect fire kiln. A type of kiln that has a heat chamber into which the air is first warmed and then ventilated through the layers of malt.

Indicator Time Test. A method for measuring the degree of oxidation of a beer. The test measures the time, in seconds, for a solution of dichloro indophenol (dichloro-2,6 phenol-indophenol-sodium) to become discolored when beer is added. In the case of beers treated with anti-oxidants, the indicator may be close to zero; non-treated beers of average density rate about 500 Indicator Time Test (or seconds); some oxidized beers may reach many thousands of seconds.

infection. Spoilage of beer by wild yeast or bacteria. The bacteria are principally members of the genera *Streptococcus - Pediococcus, Achromobacter, Lactobacillus* and *Acetobacter*.

infusion brewing method. Synonym for infusion mashing.

infusion mashing. One of the three mashing methods and the traditional method for top-fermenting beer. The process is carried out at a constant temperature and in a single vessel, a mash tun fitted with a perforated false bottom. The mash, which is not boiled, is sprayed with hot water to raise the mashing temperature gradually to 65 to 68°C (149 to 154°F) for one to two hours. After mashing is complete, the wort is drawn through the slotted base which can be opened to filter the liquid while straining the spent grains. **Syn:** infusion brewing method. Sometimes referred to as single-temperature mashing. **See also:** mashing; decoction mashing.

initial fermentation. Synonym for primary fermentation.

International Bitterness Unit. Synonym for bitterness unit.

inversion. The breakdown of sucrose into its composite monosaccharides, namely, glucose and fructose.

invert sugar. Processed common sugar (sucrose) separated into two sugars, fructose and glucose, by a modification of the molecular structure. It is obtained industrially by the inversion of sucrose with dilute acid, usually sulfuric acid, into equal parts of glucose and fructose. It does not contain dextrins and can be used as an adjunct or for priming.

invertase. An enzyme that hydrolyzes disaccharides to monosaccharides, especially sucrose into the invert sugars glucose and fructose. **Syn:** sucrase; saccharase.

iodine (starch) test. Synonym for starch test.

ion. An atom or molecule which, by loss of one or more electrons, has acquired an electric charge: **See also:** anion; cation.

IPA. Abbreviation for India pale ale.

Irish moss. A red seaweed, *Chondrus crispus*, added during the last minutes of the boiling process to help clear the beer by causing haze-forming substances to coagulate and settle out. **Syn**: carragen; carragheen moss; *Chondrus crispus*.

Irish Picon. A cocktail prepared by pouring Amer Picon and (Guinness) stout over ice in a large glass. Add a zest of lemon and serve cold.

isinglass. A gelatinous substance processed from the swimming bladder of sturgeon from American and U.S.S.R. rivers (containing 70 to 77% gelatin) and other fishes such as cod, ling and carp and added to beer for fining purposes. **Syn**: fish stuffing (U.K.); fish gelatin.

Island Grog. A cocktail prepared by heating 12 ounces of Pilsener with four coffeespoons of powdered sugar and one soupspoon of white rum. Remove from heat just before boiling and serve hot.

isohumulones. See: alpha acid.

iso-alpha-acids. See: alpha acid.

isomerized hop extract. See: hop extract.

I.T.T. Abbreviation for Indicator Time Test.

Jj

Jacob's ladder. A ladder-like conveyor for transporting ale casks from the cellar to the brewery or pub.

Jacob's ladderman. The person responsible for operating a Jacob's ladder.

Japanese rice wine. Another name for saké. Also called Japanese rice beer.

Javel water. A solution of sodium hypochlorite, NaOCl, in water, used as a bleaching agent or disinfectant. Named after *Javel*, a former French village (now part of Paris), where it was made. **See also:** chlorine.

Jenlain. A deep bronze-colored, fruity, apéritif beer brewed by top fermentation at the Brasserie Duyck in the northern French town of Jenlain, south of Valenciennes. It is full-bodied, of 20°B, filtered but not pasteurized and is sold in 75 centiliter Champagne-like corked bottles.

jetting machine. An automatic machine for washing bottles.

Jingle. A mix of ale sweetened and flavored with nutmeg and apples.

Joao Weisse. A cocktail prepared by adding one soupspoon of red port and one coffeespoon of powdered sugar to a pint of Weissbier and crushed ice. Mix slowly, sprinkle a pinch of grated nutmeg and serve cold.

jug. A vessel for holding and pouring liquids, usually deep, often pear-shaped with a bottle-type mouth closed with a cork.

Julifest Maubergeoise. Alternative name for the Kermesse de la bière de Mauberge.

Jungbukett. German for goût de jeune or unpleasant smelling green beer.

Jungfrauenbecher. A German festive drinking cup manufactured in the 16th and 17th century depicting a young lady in a long bell-shaped skirt holding a pivoting basket over her head. When the basket figure is inverted, the woman's skirt forms a first bowl and the pivoting basket forms a second, smaller one. Such cups were used at wedding feasts where the groom was expected to drink from the larger bowl, without spilling the contents of the smaller one, which he passed to the bride.

Kk

kachasu. An orthographic variant of kuchasu.

kaffir beer. The traditional beverage of the Bantu tribes of Africa. It was traditionally prepared from millet (*Panicum miliaceum*) steeped for 24 hours, packed in cloth bags to germinate for another 48 hours and then sundried. The malted grains were mashed with raw grains, brought to a boil, cooled in open air and fermented by wild yeasts. It was first brewed commercially in Salisbury in 1908 (then Rhodesia, later Zimbabwe). It is presently made, in South Africa, from fermented malted sorghum, which is known locally as kaffir corn. Elsewhere it is prepared from a mixture of malted sorghum and malted barley or, as in Nigeria, with the addition of gari, a starchy cassava preparation. The kaffir beer of South Africa is consumed by the blacks (but controlled by the whites) at a rate of 200 liters per capita per year (compared to 147 liters per year by West Germans). This beer is neither hopped nor filtered and, hence, contains large amounts of particulate matter. After initial fermentation, it is pasteurized, and a secondary fermentation is induced by priming and re-yeasting. It is sold in an active state of fermentation and officially holds 3% alcohol, but since it is still fermenting this may vary considerably. Etym.: Kaffir (from the Arabic *kafir* meaning infidel) was originally a derogatory name given to the black Bantu tribes not converted to Islam. **Syn**: Bantu beer; sorghum beer; kaffir.

kaoliang. A form of beer made from sorghum in China during the Song Dynasty (960-1278 AD). Sorghum, also called kaoliang, was cultivated in the Sechouan province.

kaulms. Synonym for culms.

kava. A sort of beer once brewed in Polynesia from the roots of a giant tree called *Piper methysticum*, the dried roots of which were chewed, spat and brewed.

keg. A small cask usually with a capacity of 10 gallons or less. In Britain, aluminum or stainless steel kegs have a 9-, 10- or 11- gallon capacity (41, 45.5 or 50 liters).

keg beer. In England, draft beer that is filtered and cooled before kegging and which will be forced out of the keg by pressurized carbon dioxide gas. It is served chilled while Real Ale is served at ambiant temperature (13.3°C or 42.6°F). **See also:** casked beer; Real Ale.

kegging. Drawing beer from a fermenter to kegs.

Kent Goldings. A variety of hops grown in England and containing about 5% alpha acids.

Kermesse de la bière de Mauberge. A beer festival started in 1961 in the town of Mauberge, France with the encouragement of the Porter 39 brewery. It is held yearly in July from noon to midnight for 12 to 16 days usually starting around the 13th. It also is known as Julifest Maubergeoise.

kettle. Synonym for brew-kettle.

khadi. A mead-like alcoholic beverage or melomel brewed in Botswana from a mixture of honey and wild berries.

kick. Synonym for punt.

kiesel. A form of beer once made from rye and oats in the Soviet Union and Central Europe. **Syn:** zur.

kieselguhr. Finely powdered sedimentary silica from the skeletons of diatoms and used for clarification or fining.

kieselguhr filter. A type of filter consisting of a thick layer of kieselguhr through which the beer is pumped.

kil(d). Abbreviation for kilderkin.

kilderkin. In England, a cask for beer with a capacity of 2 firkins or 18 imperial gallons (81.8 liters). Abbrev: kil or kild. **See also:** firkin; pin.

kiln. A large furnace with a perforated floor, formerly heated by open fire but now mostly from oil-fired heaters, through which controlled drafts of hot air dry and roast the malt. **Syn:** malt kiln.

kiln-dried hops. Hops dried in a special kiln shortly after harvesting. Freshly picked hop cones contain 75 to 80% moisture which must be reduced rapidly to 12 or 13% to prevent the soft resins and essential oils from oxidizing and polymerizing. The drying temperature should not exceed 50°C (122°F) otherwise the quality will be impaired by a loss of lupulin.

kiln fan. The rotating apparatus inside a kiln.

kiln floor. Name given to each of the platforms inside a kiln.

kilning. The process of heat-drying malted barley in a kiln to stop germination and produce a dry, easily milled malt from which the brittle rootlets are easily removed. Kilning also removes the raw flavor (or green-malt flavor) associated with germinating barley, and new aromas, flavors and colors develop according to the intensity and duration of the kilning process. Kilning results in a loss of about 30 to 60% of the enzymatic activity of the green malt as well as arresting further enzyme activity in the malt itself. Kilning is carried out in stages: a drying phase to about 10% moisture (called hand-dry malt) at 45 to 50°C (113 to 122°F) or less followed by a curing phase at 80 to 110°C (176 to 230°F) or higher when the moisture content is reduced to about 6% or, as in ale brewing, to about 2%. The temperature also affects the color of the malt husks and, consequently, the color of the beer. Pale-hued mild-tasting beers are produced by removing the malted barley immediately after drying while darker, stronger beers require a longer drying period at higher temperatures. **Syn**: drying. **See also**: melanoidins.

Kindel Berliner Weisse. See: Berliner Weisse.

kiu. Orthographic variant for chiu.

Klosterbräu. See: abbey beer.

Kölsch. A very pale, golden-hued, top-fermented beer produced in the metropolitan area of Bonn-Cologne. Under German law, when it is brewed elsewhere in Germany, the name of the locality must precede the word Kölsch. It is highly hopped, mildly alcoholic (±3.7% w/v, 4.6% v/v) and slightly lactic in taste. **Etym**: From Köln, the German name for the city of Cologne and Kölschbier, beer from that city.

korma. 1. In ancient Egypt, sweet barley wine (beer) flavored with ginger. **2.** A millet beer brewed by the Celts. Also called: corma, korma or kurmi. Compare: courni.

kraeusen. Pronounciation: kroysen. The 'rocky' or 'cauliflower' heads of foam which appear on the surface of the wort during the first days of fermentation. When they reach their peak, between the fourth and the seventh day, they are called high kraeusen or rocky heads.

kraeusened beer. A beer conditioned by kraeusening.

kraeusening. A method of conditioning that adds a small quantity of young fermenting wort (about 15 to 20%) to a fully fermented lagering one to create a secondary fermentation and natural carbonation.

Krebs cycle. Synonym for citric acid cycle. **Etym**: Named after Sir Hans Krebs, British scientist, who first studied this sequence of enzyme-catalyzed reactions.

kriek. A beer produced in Belgium by steeping Shaerbeck cherries in young lambic or gueuse to induce a new fermentation. The red cherries (called kersen) and the black cherries (called krieken), harvested in late July and early August, are added at a rate of 100 kilos per 500 liters of lambic and macerate for four to eight months. The beer is then filtered, clarified and bottled and is aged for another year. When kriek is kept over five years it gains in alcoholic strength but loses in cherry flavor. It is cherry-red, has a fine creamy foam, a bittersweet flavor and a strength of about 4.8% alcohol by weight (6.0% by volume). Most of the cherries now come from the Senne River valley or from the north of France (morello cherries). **Syn**: kriek(en)-lambic or kriekenlambic; cherry beer. **See also**: kriekenbier; lambic; gueuse; framboise.

kriekenbier. A type of beer, not to be confused with kriek, produced in Belgium by macerating cherries in top-fermented barley beer.

krupnik. An alcoholic drink made in Poland from a mix of local whiskey and honey.

Ku-Baba. A breweress and tavern-keeper who lived in Sumer in the year 2400 BC. A remarkable woman and successful brewer, she founded the city of Kish, about 20 kilometers northeast of Babylonia, eventually became sovereign of that city and founded the Third Dynasty of Kish.

kuchasu. A spirit made in Zimbabwe by distillation of a native beer. Also spelled: kachasu. Sometimes called: tileque.

Kulminator. The strongest beer in the world, a double bock of 13.2% alcohol by volume, brewed in Kulmbach in northern Bavaria, Germany.

Kupferstube. A copper-colored, bottom-fermented beer of 12.8°B brewed in Nürnberg, Franconia (Germany) the color of which is caused by the use of smoky, roasted malts.

kurunnu. A type of beer made from spelt (an early form of wheat) in ancient Babylonia.

kvas(s). A Russian beery drink, mildly alcoholic (0.2 to 2.0%), traditionally made by fermenting rye bread, one that does not include any grain but rye. The fermenting liquid will be turned bitter by oats or other grains. Kvas was brewed by the proto-Slavs as early as 2,000 years ago. The basic recipe consisted in mixing dried breadcrumbs with hot water, adding sugar solution and yeast for fermentation. The brew was flavored with raisins, mint, absinth, juniper, honey, sugar or, rarely, hops during fermentation. Wealthy people flavored their Kvas with bilberries, Morello cherries, currants, apples, lemons, pears, raspberries, lingonberries. The importation of English ales in the 18th century marked the decline of this beverage. Kvas is still produced in northern USSR. Rye bread is covered with boiling water, churned and left standing for 24 hours after which time more water and yeasts are added and the brew is fermented in casks for two to three days. It is later delivered in cistern trucks and people buy it directly from the cistern on street corners and market places. Also spelled: kwas(s); quas(s). **See also**: ioblochny; grouchevoï; malinovoï.

kwas(s). Orthographic variant for kvas(s).

l. Abbreviation for liter.

label. A piece of paper or foil glued to a bottle on which are printed various information — brand name, alcohol content, brewery, and others.

labeler. A machine for sticking labels to bottles. **Syn**: labeling machine.

labeling machine. Synonym for labeler.

lace. The lace-like pattern of bubbles sticking to a glass of beer once it has been partly or totally emptied.

lack of body. Descriptive of a thin, watery beer as opposed to a light-, medium- or full-bodied one.

lactic acid. Formula: CH_3-CHOH-COOH. A mild-flavored carboxylic acid found in milk (hence its name) and known in three forms of which the Dl-form (also known as Dl-lactic acid or ordinary lactic acid) may develop as bacteria in the mash during brewing and acidify the mash at temperatures of 40° to 47°C (113° to 116.6°F); however, lactic acid formation is more likely to occur in fermentation and aging (via infection).

lactose. A non-fermentable sugar used to add body and sweetness to stouts and brown beers.

lady's waist. In Ireland and Australia, a beer glass with a capacity of about 3 1/2 ounces (± 1 deciliters).

lagales. A term coined by beer author Howard Hillman, a contraction of the words LAGER and ALE, to describe hybrid brews produced by blending bottom-fermented lagers with top-fermented ales.

lager. A generic term for any beer produced by bottom fermentation, usually by decoction mashing, as opposed to top-fermented beers, usually produced by infusion mashing, called ales. Lager brewing was introduced in the 1840s and is now the predominant brewing method worldwide except in Britain where top fermentation is dominant. Lagers constitute a category including Münchener, Vienna, Pilsener, Dortmunder, Bock and Doppelbock. Most lagers are of the Pilsener style; they tend to be paler, crisper, drier and less alcoholic than ales. True lagers are matured (lagered) in cold storage rooms for one to three months and sometimes longer, but modern methods complete aging much more rapidly. Etym.: From the German verb and noun *Lagern*, to store or storage area. **Syn**: bottom-fermented beer. **See also**: bottom fermentation; bottom-fermenting yeast; ale.

lagered beer. A bottom-fermented beer that has matured in cold cellars for many weeks or even months at near-zero temperatures.

lagering. Storing bottom-fermented beer in cold cellars at near-zero temperatures for periods of time ranging from a few weeks to several months and occasionally up to a year, during which time the yeast cells and proteins settle out and the beer improves in taste. This technique originated in the Bavarian Alps in the 15th century and was later practiced on a larger scale in Munich, Vienna and Plzeň. **Syn**: cold lagering.

Lager Weisse. In Germany, a bottom-fermented wheat beer.

lager yeast. Synonym for bottom fermenting yeast.

lag period. Synonym for lag phase.

lag phase. Associated with yeast viability, the time elapsed between yeast pitching and the start of activity as signaled by the appearance of foam at the surface of the wort. During this time the yeast cells become larger but do not produce any buds. The time ranges from about two hours for worts of 1.010 original gravity to four hours for those of a gravity of 1.100. **Syn**: lag period. **See also**: reproduction phase.

lamb-ale. In medieval England, an ale prepared for the sheep-shearing season.

lambic. A unique Belgian wheat beer produced only in a 15-kilometer radius south-west of Brussels in the area called Pajottenland. Lambic is traditionally brewed in winter (15 October to 15 May) because, at that time, a microflora develops in the atmosphere of the Senne River valley, and because the first few months of fermentation must not be too vigorous. The mash, consisting of 60 to 70% barley and 30 to 40% wheat, is spontaneously fermented by these airborne wild yeasts (*Brettanomyces bruxellensis* and *Brettanomyces cambicus*) and bacteria (thermo bacteria and lactic bacteria). The fermentation vessels consist of large oak or chestnut tuns of 252 gallons each. Fermentation starts after three days and an attenuation of 80% is reached after the first summer and is almost complete after the second. It is flavored with old hops, because it must not be bitter, at a rate of 600 grams per hectoliter. Lambic may be served young (three months to one year) or old (at least two years old, usually three to four). Young lambic is very sour, slightly cloudy and produces little or no froth. Old lambic has lost some of its sourness, acquired a vinous bittersweet flavor and produces a fine froth. When young and old lambic are blended, bottled and aged one more year the end-product is called gueuze. In 1965 the terms lambic, gueuze and gueuze-lambic were defined by royal decree: such beers must be made by spontaneous fermentation of a wort of at least 5° Belgian (with a maximum tolerance of 5%) containing at least 30% wheat, and the packaging must bear the name of the producer and that of the place of origin. Etym.: Possibly from the French *alambic* meaning still or from the Latin *lamper*. Sometimes spelled locally: lambick. **See also:** faro; gueuze; kriek; Mort Subite; wheat beer.

Lamb's wool. A popular drink in 17th century England prepared by adding the pulp of roasted apples (five or six) together with sugar, grated nutmeg and a pinch of ginger to one quart (or three quarts) of warm strong ale. Also spelled: Lambswool.

last running. The last of the wort to be filtered from the straining vat.

Late Cluster. A variety of hops grown in Idaho and Washington containing 5.5 to 7.5% alpha acids.

late hopping. In homebrewing, the addition of aroma hops ten to twenty minutes before the end of the boil.

latent heat. The amount of heat required for a liquid to vaporize.

lauter. Name given to the mash once saccharification is complete.

lauter tun. A large vessel fitted with a false slotted bottom and a drain spigot in which the mash is allowed to settle and the grains are removed from the sweet wort through a straining process. In smaller breweries and in the infusion system the mash tun is used for both mashing and lautering. **Syn:** lauter tub.

lautering. The process of separating the spent grains from the sweet wort with a straining apparatus. Etym: From the German *lauter* meaning clarifying.

leaven. The name given to yeast in the Old and New Testaments and later applied to any substance that could cause fermentation such as barm, yeast, baking powder or sour milk.

lees. The sediments of yeast, bacteria and other solid matter that accumulate on the bottom of fermentation vessels or storage containers.

Lemon Shandy. See: Shandy Gaff.

Leuven Bier Festival. A beer festival held annually at Whitsuntide (12-15 May) in the town of Louvain in Belgium.

Leuvense Wit. Synonym for blanche de Louvain.

li. A type of rice beer made in China during the Han Dynasty (200 BC) at the beginning of the Chinese Empire. **See also:** shu; chiu; t'ien tsiou.

lickspigot. Obsolete British slang for an ale-house keeper.

life expectancy. Synonym for shelf life.

light ale. 1. In Britain, a beer of lighter color than mild ale or one slightly less alcoholic than pale ale. 2. A bottled version of bitter, hence, a synonym for pale ale.

Light-and-Mild. A mix of equal parts of pale ale and mild ale.

light beer. 1. In America, a low-calorie beer containing no dextrin. Such beers are often advertised as "less filling" or "less fattening." Light beers contain about 90 to 160 calories per bottle. **See also:** diet beer. 2. In America, a low-alcohol beer ranging from 2.3 to 3.2% alcohol by weight (2.8 to 4.0% by volume). 3. In Europe and America, a pale beer, usually a lager, as opposed to a dark one.

lightstruck. An unpleasant flavor in beer caused by exposure to light causing undesirable chemical reactions of hydrogen sulfide and other sulfur compounds with a side chain of the isohumulones and the formation of phenyl mercaptan (3-methyl-2-butene-1-thiol), which impart a skunk-like flavor. **Syn:** sunstruck.

limit attenuation. Synonym for final degree of attenuation.

lion. In France, a beer glass with a capacity of 40 centiliters. **See also:** demi; distingué; botte.

lipid. Any of a class of compounds that contains long-chain aliphatic hydrocarbons and their derivatives; includes fats and waxes. In the brewing process, lipids inhibit foam stability and, upon decomposition, contribute stale flavors. Also spelled: lipoid.

lipoid. Orthographic variant for lipid.

liquefaction. **See:** dextrinization.

liquefying enzyme. Synonym for alpha-amylase.

liquid pint. **See:** pint.

liquor. The name given, in the brewing industry, to water used for mashing and brewing, especially natural or treated water containing large amounts of calcium and magnesium salts. **Syn:** brewing water; mashing liquor; brewing liquor. **See also:** brewing water.

lite beer. An American spelling for light beer.

liter. A metric unit of volume. It is defined as the volume of one kilogram of pure water at 4°C. It is equal to about 1.76 imperial pints or 2.113 U.S. pints. Abbrev: l or L.

logarithmic phase. Synonym for reproduction phase.

long glass. Synonym for yard-of-ale.

loose hops. Hops picked from the vine and packaged without further processing other than separating the leaves from the cones after drying. **Syn**: whole hops. **See also**: pocket.

loss in yield. The loss in weight and yield during the various stages of the beermaking process. The scientific study of these phenomena (beer loss, malting loss) is intended to increase efficiency and maximize the yield.

low-alcohol(ic) beer. Synonym for near beer.

low-cal beer. An abbreviated form for low-calorie beer.

low-calorie beer. A beer of low caloric content in which the dextrins have been converted by amyloglucosidase. Abbrev: low-cal beer. **See also**: light beer; diet beer.

low fermentation. A synonym for bottom fermentation.

luda. The name given to beer by the Ossets (or Ossetians), a Caucasian tribe of Aryan tongue and Iranian descent. Spring barley was called *kheri* and hops were called *suah*. The Ossets are credited for having built a 600-liter beer reservoir, the largest in antiquity. It was discovered in Tappakallah and dates back to 600 BC. The Ossets' toast was "Dazaranbon Danasa," which translates into "I drink to your health." Also spelled: ludi.

lug. A kind of protruding handle on a vase or vessel.

Lunatic broth. **See**: old ale.

lupomaniac. A term coined by beer author Terry Foster for a "hop fanatic," one who appreciates a well hopped beer and does not believe in the expression "too hoppy."

lupulin. What appearrs as finely granular yellow powder at the base of each flower petal of the hop cone. It contains essential oils and bitter resins that impart bitterness and aromatic flavor to beer along with a sterilizing quality Once called: hop flour. **See also**: hops; hop oils; soft resins; alpha acid; beta acids.

lupulin gland. The gland (about 0.1 mm in diameter) at the base of the bracteole of the female flower in which the bitter resins and essential oils of the hop plant develop.

lupulon(e). Synonym for beta acid, one of the two resins found in hops, composed of lupulone, colupulone and adlupulone.

Lupus salictarius. The name given by Pliny the Elder (23 AD) and his contemporaries to hops and meaning "wolf among scrubs" because hops then grew wild among willows like a wolf in the forest. The botanical name for hops, Humulus lupulus, has derived from this expression.

Lüttje Lage. A German word meaning "small one" referring to a "small beer" brewed especially for the Schutzenfest (sharpshooter's festival). It is usually accompanied by a Korn (schnapps) not in the beer-chaser style but to be drunk simultaneously, the smaller glass held above the larger one, both liquids blending in the pouring and drinking process.

L-xyloascorbic acid. Synonym for ascorbic acid.

Mm

maas. An old Alsatian capacity measure estimated at 1.63 liters.

Madagascar gum. Synonym for agar-agar.

Madureira. A cocktail consisting of Pilsener and Madeira wine served chilled in a tall glass.

maize. A grain (from Zea mays) used as an adjunct mostly for top-fermenting beers. Flaked maize does not need to be pre-boiled but whole maize first must be degermed to remove the oily embryo. Maize flour contains 12 to 13% moisture, 63% starch and 9% protein. Syn: Indian corn. See also: flaked maize.

maize meal. Ground maize, not to be confused with maize flour, which is better known as corn flour.

malinovoï. Kvas in which raspberries have macerated.

malt, to. To convert barley into malt.

malt. Processed barley that has been steeped in water, germinated on malting floors or in germination boxes or drums and later dried in kilns for the purpose of converting the insoluble starch in barley to the soluble substances and sugars in malt. Three factors determine the value of good malt: (1) its protein content must be as low as possible (preferably below 12.8%), (2) its starch content must be as high as possible, (3) its germinative power must be superior to 98%. Syn: malted barley. See also: malting; black (patent) malt; caramel malt; crystal malt; dextrin malt; Münich malt; pale malt; toasted malt.

Composition of Barley and Malt (percentage dry weight)		
	Barley	**Malt**
Starch	63-65	58-60
Sucrose	1-2	3-5
Reducing sugars	0.1-0.2	3-4
Other sugars	1.0-1.2	2-4
Soluble gums	1.0-1.5	2-4
Hemicelluloses	8-10	6-8
Cellulose	4-5	5
Lipids (fats)	2-3	2-3
Protein (nitrogen x 6.25)	8-11	8-11
Amino acids and peptides	0.5	1-2
Nucleic acids	0.2-0.3	0.2-0.3
Mineral salts	2	2.2
Other substances	5-6	6-7

Source: G. Harris. *Barley and Malt*, p. 435. Edited by A.H. Cook, Academic Press, 1962.

malt adjunct. Synonym for adjunct.

maltase. An enzyme responsible for the transformation of maltose to dextrose.

malt beer. Usually refers to nutritious malt beverages of very low alcohol content brewed originally for nursing mothers and children and now enjoyed by sportsmen and health-concious people. In France it is called *bière de malt* and in Germany *Malzbier*.

malt beverage. Any alcoholic or non-alcoholic beverage made from malted barley.

malt cleaning machine. An apparatus consisting of a perforated metal drum used to degerminate (remove the rootlets) malted barley.

malt comes. Synonym for malt tails.

malt crusher. Synonym for grinder.

malted. 1. Converted into malt. 2. Treated with or made from malt.

malted barley. Synonym for malt.

malt extract. 1. A thick, sugary syrup or dry powder prepared from malt. Basically it is sweet wort reduced to a syrup or powder form by removing most or all of the water by low vacuum evaporation and packaged in cans of 2, 2.2, 2.5, 3, 3.3 or 3.5 pounds. **See also:** wet kit; dry kit. 2. A dark and thick beer-like malt drink of low alcohol content.

malt floor. In traditional-style maltings, a flat horizontal surface area where steeped barley grains are spread in layers of 10 to 15 centimeters to germinate. Because they require considerable space malting floors have been replaced by mechanical devices such as the germination box. **Syn:** malting floor.

malt heap. The uniform layer of malt on the malt floor. **Syn:** couches.

malthouse. A building where barley is converted into malt.

malting. The process of converting barley into malt. It is divided into three stages: **1.** steeping, the barley is immersed in water until a chosen moisture level has been reached; **2.** germination, the wet barley is allowed to germinate under controlled conditions; **3.** kilning, the germinated barley (green malt) is heat-dried and partly cooked.

malting floor. Synonym for malt floor.

maltings. The buildings in which malt is processed.

malt hopper. A funnel-like apparatus for channeling the dried malt to the mill.

malt kiln. Synonym for kiln.

malt liquor. **1.** Generally speaking, a beer of higher alcohol content than regular beer. **2.** In America, an alternative name given to beers that exceed the alcohol level defined by law and which are therefore too alcoholic to be labeled lager or beer. On the average they contain 4.5 to 6.0% alcohol by weight (5.6 to 7.5% v/v) as contrasted to the 3.2 to 4.0% (4.0 to 5.0% v/v) in regular beers.

maltman. Synonym for maltster.

maltmaster. Synonym for maltster.

malt mill. Synonym for grinder.

malt oar. Synonym for turner.

maltobiose. Synonym for maltose.

maltodextrin. A general name for compounds of maltose and dextrins formed by the diastatic hydrolysis of starch during saccharification.

maltogenic amylase. Synonym for beta amylase.

maltose. Formula: $C_{12}H_{22}O_{11}$. A fermentable sugar consisting of two molecules (disaccharide) of glucose obtained by the enzymatic hydrolysis of starch. It is water soluble and 33% as sweet as sucrose. **Syn:** malt sugar; maltobiose.

malt plow. An instrument or apparatus for turning the germinating barley on the malt floor.

malt polisher. An apparatus consisting of two revolving brushes used for polishing the malt.

malt screen. A sieve with the double purpose of removing dust, sand and stones while grading the grains.

malt sprouts. Synonym for rootlets.

maltster. A person who makes malt. **Syn:** maltman; maltmaster.

malt sugar. Synonym for maltose.

malt tails. The bearded chaff removed from the drying or dried malt and used as fodder or fertilizer. **Syn:** malt comes; beard.

malt tannins. Tannins derived from the malt husks as opposed to hop tannins. **See also:** tannin.

malt-to-sugar ratio. In homebrewing, the maximum amount of sugar that can be added to the boiling wort or malt extract without affecting taste. This ratio preferably should be less than two to one.

malt worm. Synonym for grain weevil. Scientific name: *Calandra granaria*.

malty. 1. Displaying the characteristic flavor of malt. 2. Related to malt.

Malzbier. In Germany, a dark, sweet, aromatic malt beverage containing only 0.5 to 1.5% alcohol by weight. Not a true beer but rather a tonic once brewed for children and nursing mothers but now enjoyed by sportsmen and health-conscious people. Examples include: Mumme, Karamalz, Vitamalz. **See also:** near beer; bière de malt; malt beer.

manioc. See: tapioca.

manioc beer. An alcoholic drink made from the Manihot plant. The first description of such a beer produced by the Tupi cannibal tribes of the coastal regions of Brazil dates back to Hans Staden, *Véritable histoire et description d'un pays habité...* written in 1557. The Tupinamba tribes were decimated in the 17th and 18th century but manioc beer is still the daily and sacred beverage in Amazonia and the favorite drink of the Jivaros. **Syn:** cassava beer.

Märzen(bier). 1. In Germany, before the advent of artificial refrigeration, beer was brewed in winter and the last batch, brewed in March, was made especially strong to survive the many months of maturation before it was drunk at the end of summer. 2. The name given by Josef Sedlmayr, owner of the Zum Franziskanerkeller, to a Vienna-style bottom-fermented blond beer he invented in 1871 in contrast to the brown beers then popular in Bavaria. The first batch was brewed in March 1872, hence, the name March beer, and was served for the first time at the Oktoberfest of the same year. Today's Märzenbiers, still a favorite of the Oktoberfest, contain about 4.5% alcohol by weight (as opposed to 3.5 to 3.9% for ordinary pale beers called *helles*) and are fermented at an original wort gravity of 12.5 to 13.0°B. 3. Because of the similarities in style of the two beers, the terms Vienna and Märzen are sometimes synonymous.

mash, to. To mix ground malt with hot water. **Syn:** to dough-in.

mash. 1. A mixture of ground barley malt and hot water that forms the sweet wort after straining. **2.** Synonym for mash goods.

mash copper. Synonym for mash kettle.

masher. A container into which grist and water are mixed.

mash filter. A filter press fitted with either cloth or plates for filtering the mash.

mash goods. 1. The portion of wort that is boiled separately in the decocting brewing method. **2.** The total amount of barley required for a single brew. **Syn**: mash.

mashing. The process of mixing ground malt with water in the mash tun to extract the malt, degrade haze-forming proteins and further convert grain starches to fermentable sugars and non-fermentable carbohydrates (dextrins) that will add body, head retention and other characteristics to the beer. This conversion is operated by the hydrolytic action of endogenous enzymes, mainly alpha and beta amylases. Alpha amylases convert insoluble and solubilized starch into maltotriose and dextrins; beta amylases then convert dextrins into glucose, maltose, maltotriose and limit dextrins; and invertase hydrolyzes saccharose into glucose and fructose. The whole process is carried out in one of three ways: **1.** infusion mashing, in a single vessel, at 65 to 68°C (149 to 154°F) as for ales; **2.** decoction mashing, by boiling portions of the mash in a separate vessel to raise the temperature from 45 to 76°C (113 to 168°F) as for lagers; **3.** mixed mashing, a combination of the infusion and decoction methods. Mashing requires several hours (one to seven) and produces a sugar-rich liquid called sweet wort. **See also**: infusion mashing; decoction mashing.

mashing-in. Synonym for doughing-in.

mashing liquor. Synonym for liquor.

mashing time. The period of time required for infusion or decoction mashing.

mashing tun. Synonym for mash tun.

mash kettle. The metal vat into which part of the mash is boiled for the decoction brewing method. **Syn**: mash copper.

mash rest. Maintaining the mashing temperature at a specific level ideal for certain desired enzymatic reactions. **Syn**: strike temperature.

mash tub. Synonym for mash tun.

mash tun. A large vessel for holding the mash, usually made of copper, brass or stainless steel. The mash tuns used for infusion mashing are fitted with a perforated false bottom and a system of pipes for drawing off the wort and sparging machinery for washing the spent grains. Mash tuns used for decoction mashing are fitted with a propeller or stirrer at the rounded bottom and have a dome with a sliding door and a chimney for the evacuation of steam at the top. **Syn**: mashing tun; mash tub.

mash-tun rake. A rake with claws to cut and remove dregs.

mass filter. A type of filter consisting of layers of pressed pulp fitted into perforated frames through which beer is pumped under pressure. **Syn:** pulp filter.

Masskrug. In Germany, a beer mug with a capacity of one liter. **See also:** Halbe.

master-brewer. 1. An expert brewer. 2. One who supervises the brewing operations in a brewery. **Syn:** head-brewer; brew-master; brewmaster.

matted couche. Malting barley that has not been turned at the proper time resulting in long intermixed radicles. **See also:** couch; mat plow; radicle; turner.

maturation. The improvement of the quality of beer by aging in a storage container at near zero temperatures for lagers and around 4.4 to 7.2°C (40 to 45°F) for ales during which time the yeast cells precipitate and the finished beer acquires a smooth, mellow flavor. **Syn:** maturing; aging.

maturing. Is said of a beer in the process of aging.

mead. An alcoholic beverage produced by fermenting honey and water. Mead can by dry, sweet or sparkling. **Etym:** From the Indo-European spelling *medhu* later derived into met, med, meda, meath. **Syn:** honey wine. **See also:** black mead; cyser; metheglin; melomel; pyment; hippocras; red mead.

meadmaker. A person who makes mead.

meadery. An establishment where mead is made.

mealie beer. A beer brewed in South Africa from maize or millet and other plants.

measure. Capacity vessel of standard size used for measuring liquids. The Imperial system of measures was introduced in 1824. **See also:** conversion table at the end of the book.

medicinal. Synonym for phenolic.

medicinal beer. **See:** brutolé.

melanoidins. Dark colored (brown or black) organic compounds which form during kilning and kettle boil through a complex series of chemical reactions (called Maillard reactions) involving amino acids and sugars. Dark malts are colored by melanoidins.

melibiose. Formula: $C_{12}H_{22}O_{11}$. A naturally occurring disaccharide based on 6(alpha-D galactoside)-D-glucose; a reducing sugar.

mellow. Descriptive of a beer that is sweet and soft in taste, not irritating.

melomel. Any mead in which part of the honey has been replaced by crushed fruits or fruit juices. **Syn:** fruit mead. **See also:** black mead; cyser; pyment; red mead.

meniscus. The slight curvature of liquid adhering to glass objects caused by surface tension. Also called: meniscus effect.

merissa. See: bilbil.

Mertzbier. A type of beer brewed in 1763 in Strasbourg, Alsace. It was so named because it was brewed in winter time in the best of conditions and served in March after several months of maturation in cold cellars.

metallic. Possessing an undesirable taste of metal.

methanol. Synonym for methyl alcohol.

metheglin. Any mead flavored with herbs and spices. Etym: From the Welsh words medclydlin and meddyglyn meaning medicine. **See also**: sack metheglin.

methyl alcohol. Formula: CH_3OH. A highly toxic alcohol; the first member of the alcohol series. **Syn**: methanol; wood alcohol.

methylated alcohol. Ethyl alcohol denatured with methyl alcohol.

méthode Champenoise. In France and Belgium, a method for conditioning Champagne and, occasionally, beer by inducing a secondary fermentation in the bottle.

methylene blue. A blue dye used in laboratory tests to determine the number of dead yeast cells (which are stained blue) in a yeast sample. Living cells do not stain because their plasma membrane is impermeable to the dye. The test solution usually contains 0.01% methylene blue and 2% sodium citrate.

micromalting. Small-scale malting in a laboratory to determine the germinative power, dormancy and best suitable steeping and germination procedure to apply to a particular type or batch of barley.

middy. In Australia, a beer glass with a capacity of 10 ounces in New South Wales and 7 ounces in Western Australia.

mild. Describes a smooth, well-balanced beer lacking harshness or excessive bitterness.

mild ale. In Britain, a dark brown top-fermented beer, light to medium bodied, malty, sweet and lightly hopped, more or less contrasted by bitter ale. It is prepared from an original wort gravity of 1.030 to 1.036 (8 to 9°B) and may be bottled or casked but is best appreciated as a draft beer. It is served mainly in the East and West Midlands and the north-west of England.

Mild-and-Bitter. A mix of equal parts of mild and bitter ales.

Milk Ale. A cocktail prepared as follows: one liter of ale is heated in a pan with one coffeespoon of sugar, a pinch of powdered ginger and a pinch of grated nutmeg. One liter of milk is heated to boiling point in a separate vessel and added to the ale.

Milk of amnesia. See: old ale.

milk stout. Synonym for sweet stout.

mill, to. To grind malt into grist. **Syn**: to grind.

mill. Synonym for grinder.

millet. General name for the cereal from various species of *Gramineae*, all of which have a fibrous root system and rather small grains (smaller than wheat or rice).

millet beer. A type of beer once brewed in Africa. The germinated millet grains were dried and ground, boiled for twelve hours, filtered and boiled again many times before fermentation.

milliliter. One thousandth of a liter. Abbrev: ml.

milling. In malting, the malt is ground into grist (or meal) to facilitate the extraction of sugars and other soluble substances during the mashing process. The endosperm must be crushed to medium-size grits rather than to flour consistency. It is important that the husks remain intact when the grain is milled or cracked because they will later act as a filter aid during lautering. **Syn**: grinding.

millipore filtration. A type of filtration process sometimes used instead of pasteurization.

misérable. An old French capacity measure equal to half a *posson* or one-sixteenth of a pint.

mitaca. See: chicha.

mixed brewing method. Synonym for mixed mashing.

mixed mashing. A cross between the infusion and the decoction brewing methods. It is used, for example, in Belgium for the preparation of lambic and other wheat beers, where the wheat is boiled in a separate vessel while the malt is mashed by the infusion process. **Syn**: mixed brewing method.

ml. Abbreviation for milliliter.

modification. 1. The physical and chemical changes occurring in barley during malting. Physically, the grain is rendered millable. Chemically, complex molecules are broken down to simpler, soluble ones by the formation of hydrolytic enzymes which later begin to catalyze the hydrolytic degradation of the starchy endosperm and its cell walls. **2.** The degree to which malt has been converted during the malting process as determined by the extent of the growth of the acrospire.

modified. Is said of malt to describe the extent of the modification process. American malts are usually under-modified while European, especially English malts are fully modified. **See also**: under-modified; fully modified.

Moenen. In Belgium, especially in the hop-growing region of Asse, a mythical hop demon (*diable du houblon*) blamed for bad crops, bugs, diseases and all other evils victimizing the poor hop farmer. In winter he chases drunk farmers out of the pole storage shed; in spring he plagues young plants with bad spells; in summer he causes hop plants to fall to the ground; and in autumn, just before harvest, he is captured.

monastery beer. Synonym for abbey beer.

monosaccharide. A carbohydrate consisting of a single chain of carbon atoms with a hydroxyl group on all carbons (except the aldehic or ketonic carbons). Monosaccharides cannot be reduced to simpler forms by hydrolysis. Their name end with the suffix -ose (maltose, sucrose, dextrose, glucose, galactose, etc.) and are classified according to the number of carbon atoms as triose (3), tetrose (4), pentose (5), hexose (6), and heptose (7).

Moor's head. A type of hop strainer used in small breweries consisting of a cone pierced with numerous holes.

Moreau Index. A method used to identify pure varieties of hops. The index is calculated by counting the number of nodes (n) in one hundred stigs (or rachis) and measuring the length (l) in centimeters. The ratio 10 n/l gives the value of the Moreau Index. The results are plotted on a graph and compared with curves of existing hop varieties.

Morellenbier. A type of beer once brewed in the Belgian province of Limbourg by adding morello cherries to fermenting wort.

Mort Subite. 1. The name of a famous Belgian café located, in 1910, at the corner of Assaut and Montagne streets in Brussels. The café, owned by Théophile Vossen, was then called La Cour Royale. Its clientele — brokers, civil servants and bank clerks — played a game of dice called 421 in a *pitjesbak* (an octagonal wooden box 40-cm wide and 10-cm high). The loser was said to be dead but if he had to leave suddenly, he was "suddenly dead"; hence, the expression sudden death (*mort subite*). In 1927, the café moved to a new location (7 rue Montagne-aux-Herbes) and was renamed Mort Subite. 2. The name of a famous gueuze produced by the De Keersmaeker brewery of Kobbegem and served at that café. **See also:** gueuze.

Mother-in-Law. A mix of equal parts of stout and bitter ale.

mouthfeel. Synonym for body. Also spelled: mouth-feel.

mug. A drinking vessel or cup, made of various materials, usually cylindrical or baluster-shaped with a base rim and a plain or scroll handle.

mughouse. In England, an early form of the Victorian and Edwardian music hall where only men were admitted and only stout and ale were served. In it was a large room presided by a chairman, with a harpist at one end, in which members sang in turn or made speeches or toasts. **Syn:** mugroom.

mugroom. Synonym for mughouse.

mull. In England, a mix of hot ale with sugar and spices (often ginger) and sometimes other ingredients such as eggs, traditionally heated with a red-hot poker.

muller. A vessel for preparing mull.

multum. A preparation of quassia and licorice once used to adulterate beer.

mum. A strong, non-hopped ale brewed in Braunschweig (Germany) in the 18th century and apparently first brewed by Christian Mumme in the late 15th century (ca 1487). Not to be confused with Mumme, a Malzbier brewed in Germany. Also spelled: mumm.

Münchener. A bottom-fermented beer produced in the Bavarian city of Munich since the mid-19th century. The original Münchener was dark. In 1928, the Paulaner Brewery introduced a paler version, called Helles, that has almost entirely overtaken the darker brew. Both versions, helles Bier (or Munich pale lager) and dunkel Bier (or Munich dark lager), are lightly hopped (180 to 200 grams per hectoliter), distinctively malty because of the use of Munich malt and have an alcohol content of about 3.5 to 4.0% by weight (4.4 to 5.0% v/v). Munich-style beers brewed outside Germany are always dark. **Syn:** Munich (beer); Münchner.

Munich (beer). Munich-style beer (Münchener in German).

Munich malt. Malted barley kilned at slightly higher temperatures than pale malt but for a shorter period of time. It imparts sweetness, roundness of flavor and a reddish hue to such beers as Oktoberfest and Killian's Irish Red.

murbimeter. An apparatus for measuring the hardness of barley and malt grains.

mutchkin. A Scottish capacity measure for liquids equal to half a Scottish chopin (0.425 liter, 3/4 of an English pint, or 0.9 United States pint).

Nn

natural conditioning. A secondary fermentation occurring in the maturing vat when the brew still contains live yeast cells.

near beer. A malt beverage having a very low alcoholic content, usually around 0.5 to 2.0% by volume. During Prohibition, these beers were produced by distilling or cooking the alcohol out of the beer. In America, near beers must contain less than 0.5% alcohol by weight. In Germany the alcohol limit is 0.6%. Examples include Moussy, Panther, St. Christopher, Metbrew, Vita-Stout, Near Beer, Malta and Birrell. In Czechoslovakia, a non-alcoholic beer is called PROMO, a near bear is called PITO (0.5% v/v) and true beer is called PIVO. **Syn:** low-alcohol(ic) beer.

neck. The upper, narrow part of a bottle immediately below the mouth.

nephelometer. An apparatus for measuring the turbidity (haze) in liquids. The test is carried out at 70°C (158°F) because the wort invariably throws a haze upon cooling. Some instruments are graduated in Formazin Turbidity Units (or Formazin Haze Units) while others have their own standards such as degrees Nephelos (°N) on the Coleman Nephelometer. **See also:** EBC test.

neutralize, to. To render a solution neutral, i.e., neither acid nor alkaline. The pH of a neutral solution is 7.0.

Nidaba. The goddess of beer in ancient Babylonia.

Nin-Bi. The goddess of beer in ancient Sumeria. **See also:** sikaru.

Ninkasi. The Sumerian goddess of beer, "the lady who fills the mouth." In Sumeria (3600 BC) eight types of beer were produced from barley and another eight from an early type of wheat. Also spelled: Nin Ka Si.

Ninurta. The Babylonian goddess of wheat and barley.

nip. In England, a small bottle for beer and other drinks with a capacity of half a reputed pint (28.4 centiliter). Also spelled: nyp. **Syn:** split.

nog. A strong beer produced in East Anglia.

noggin. A small drinking vessel of about one quarter of a pint (0.118 liter). **See also:** pony.

non-alcoholic beer. Any malt beverage similiar in taste to beer. Not to be confused with near beer (or low-alcohol beer), which may contain up to 2.0% alcohol by volume. **Syn:** alcohol-free beer.

nondeposit beer. Synonym for chillproof beer.

non-flocculating yeast. 1. A generic name for yeast strains that do not form clumps and flocculate during fermentation. **Syn:** non-flocculent yeast. 2. A bottom-fermenting yeast of high attenuation that turns into dust during the break.

non-flocculent yeast. Synonym for non-flocculating yeast.

non-hopped. Said of a beer or malt extract not flavored with hops. **Syn:** unhopped.

non-returnable packaging. Packaging material to be disposed of after use.

Northern Brewer. 1. A variety of hops grown in Kent, England, containing 8.5 to 11.0% alpha acids. It also is grown in Washington and Oregon with an alpha acid content of 9.5 to 10.5% and a beta acid content of 4.5 to 5.5%. 2. The title of a periodical published by the Canadian Amateur Brewers Association.

nose. A taster's descriptive for the total fragrance, aroma and bouquet of a beer.

Nugget. A variety of hops grown in Oregon and containing 9.6 to 13.0% alpha acids.

nutrients. 1. The necessary elements, mainly nitrogen and phosphorous, required for the health and growth of yeast during fermentation. 2. An additive containing these elements added to the wort after pitching the yeast to assist fermentation and keep yeasts healthy.

Nuts-and-Bolts. In England, especially in East Anglia, a mix of mild and bitter.

nyp. Orthographic variant for nip.

Oo

oafka. A synonym for tiswin.

oats. A cereal grain from any plant of the genus *Avena* in the *Gramineae* family.

oatmeal. Ground oats.

off-flavor. An unpleasant flavor that develops in bottled or canned beer during storage. Carbonyls for the most part are responsible for off-flavors. **Syn:** stale flavor; aged flavor; oxidized flavor.

off-scent. A sour, grassy, stale or musty smell in beer.

O.G. Abbreviation for original gravity.

oils. See: hop oils; essential oils.

oil of barley. Slang expression for beer.

okolehao. A mildly alcoholic fermented beverage brewed by ancient Hawaiians. The root of the sacred Ti plant is baked in an underground oven, transforming the root into a molasses-like sugar that is used as a fermentable. Also called Oke.

okole maluna. A Hawaiian toast meaning "bottoms up." (Okole means "your buns" or "your rear or bottom.")

Oktoberfest. **1.** A beer festival held annually in Münich's Theresienwiese (Theresa's meadow) for sixteen days and nights in late September and early October. The festival originated with the wedding festivities of the Bavarian heir prince Ludwig to the princess Theresa in 1810. **2.** A bottom-fermented Vienna- or Märzen-style beer originally brewed especially for the Oktoberfest but now available year round. Oktoberfest beer, brewed from an original wort gravity of 1.050 to 1.060 (12.5 to 15.0°B) is copper-colored, malty and sweet.

ol. Scandinavian for beer.

old ale. In Britain, a strong, dark-colored draft beer usually prepared from an original wort gravity of 1.055 to 1.065 and sometimes higher. Such ales are sometimes described as Lunatic broth, Milk of amnesia or Chateau collapse-o.

Old Boy. A name given in 18th century England to a strong ale.

omalofo. A type of beer once brewed in Southwest Africa from kaffir corn (millet of the *Panicum miliaceum* type). Possibly a synonym for kaffir.

omm bilbil. Synonym for bilbil.

open fire kiln. A type of kiln in which cool air mixed with combusting gas is fanned into the layers of malt.

ordinary bitter. Bitter ale prepared from an original wort gravity of 1.040 to 1.048. **See also**: bitter.

Ordre du Houblon. An order founded by Jean Sans Peur, duke of Burgundy, in 1409 to honor those brewers who brewed hopped beer. The insignia of the order carried the arms of Flanders with (in the center) a gold lion surrounded by a crown of hop leaves and flowers. The listel carried the Flemish motto *Ich zuighe* meaning I savour.

original gravity. The specific gravity of the wort prior to fermentation at the temperature under consideration as compared to the density of water at 4°C (39°F), which is conventionally given the value 1.000. It is a measure of the total amount of solids that are dissolved in the wort. Abbrev: O.G. **Syn**: starting gravity; starting specific gravity; original wort gravity. **See also**: terminal gravity

original wort. Synonym for first wort.

osmophilic yeast. Having a high sugar tolerance, as yeast of the genus *Zygosaccharomyces*. Etym: from the Greek *osmos* (meaning pushing) plus *philic*.

overgrown malt. Synonym for husky grain.

outcrop. Synonym for crop.

overcarbonation. Excessive effervescence. In homebrewing, over-priming causes bottles to explode or the foam to overflow when the bottle is uncapped.

over-hopped. A very bitter beer produced by adding too much hops. **See also**: under-hopped.

over-priming. In home-brewing, adding too much sugar to the beer before putting into bottles or kegs causing the formation of excessive carbon dioxide which, in turn, is responsible for bottle explosions and gushing.

oversteeping. A prolonged steeping period causing excessive absorption of water. Oversteeping delays the onset of germination and encourages the formation and growth of mold and bacteria.

ox-horn cup. A rare synonym for drinking horn.

oxidation. **1.** A chemical reaction in which one of the reactants (beer, food) undergoes the addition of oxygen. **2.** Exposure to oxygen.

oxidized flavor. Synonym for off-flavor.

Pp

P. Abbreviation for Plato (°P).

Pa-e-bi. In pre-dynastic Mesopotamia (3000 BC), the official brewer who prepared beer for the royal family and the court.

package. A general term for containers used to market beverages. Beer is packaged in three forms: bottles, cans and kegs (barrels or casks). **Syn:** packaging.

packaging. Synonym for package.

pachwaï. The name given in northern India to a type of saké to which Cannabis sativa is added.

pale. A light-colored beer. The term is less confusing, in this sense, than light which also may refer to alcoholic or caloric content.

pale ale. In England, an amber- or copper-colored, top-fermented beer brewed with very hard water and pale malts; the bottled equivalent of bitter but drier, hoppier and lighter. The adjective pale in this instance is in distinction of darker brews such as brown ale, stout and porter. Pale ales are brewed from original wort gravities of 1.043 to 1.053 (11 to 14°B) and contain about 3.4% alcohol by volume. Classics of this style include Bass Pale and Worthington's White Shield. Pale ales are sometimes called Burton ales because the popularity of this style of beer originated from the versions brewed in Burton-on-Trent in the 1780s. **Syn:** light ale. Rarely called: dinner ale. **See also:** India pale ale.

pale crystal malt. A form of crystal malt used with pale beers; it is prepared by drying green malt at high temperature after saccharification but without curing. Larger amounts than 10% impart a disagreeable flavor to the beer. **Syn:** cara-pils.

pale malt. The most common form of malt used in brewing; pale colored malts are dried at about 80°C (176°F).

pallet. A wood frame on which crates of bottles or casks are stacked for ease of handling fork lifts.

panaché. In France, a mix of equal parts of beer and lemonade. **See also:** Shandy Gaff.

papain. A proteolytic sulfahydryl enzyme obtained from the juice of the papaya fruit. It is activated by oxidation and degrades most protein fractions, thus preventing and dissolving haze without affecting foam stability. The use of papain preparations as a chillproofing additive was first patented by Wallerstein in 1911 and is now very common.

parachute. A conical device fitted at the side or in the middle of the fermentation vessel to recover top yeast froth. The yeast, overflowing from the edge of the parachute, falls down a tube and into a receiving vessel called a yeast back. This device is now largely superseded by suction tubes that pull the yeast froth from the surface to the yeast back. **See also:** skimming oar.

parfait. In France, a one liter glass for beer.

particulate matter. Particles of various nature — protein, yeast cells and others — in suspension in a liquid.

parts per million. **See:** ppm.

party barrel. In England, a small ale barrel of 5- or 10-liter capacity, for parties, celebrations or festivities.

Pasteur effect. The conversion of an anaerobic pathway into an aerobic one occurring, for example, when beer is racked before the end of fermentation, thus introducing air into the anaerobic phase.

pasteurization. The application of intense heat to bottled, canned or kegged beer for a specific period of time for the purpose of stabilizing it biologically by killing microorganisms, germs and bacteria, stopping fermentation and prolonging shelf life. Pasteurization can be accomplished by one of two methods: in bulk, prior to bottling, by plates of tube pasteurizers activated by hot water or steam, or individually by gradually heating packaged beer up to 60 to 75°C (140 to 167°F) for 20 to 30 minutes. Draft beer is pasteurized by flash heating for 20 to 30 seconds. In Germany, export beers only are pasteurized. In England, cask-conditioned ales are, by definition, not pasteurized. Etym: After Louis Pasteur. **See also:** flash pasteurization; tunnel pasteurization.

Pasteurization Unit. A unit measuring the lethal effect (biological destruction) produced by pasteurization. It is defined as a one-minute exposure at 60°C (140°F). Bottled beer is usually pasteurized at 15 to 30 PU. Abbrev: PU or P.U.

pasteurizer. An apparatus for pasteurizing liquids.

peg tankard. A type of communal tankard popular in the late 17th century fitted with a row of pegs, usually eight, inside the drum on the handle side, each peg marking an individual share. The number of pegs varies according to the size of the tankard: a two-quart tankard had eight pegs each indicating one gill of liquid. This practice may have originated from a royal decree issued by King Edward and suggested by the Archbishop Dunstan of Canterbury in 959-975 in an effort to restrain heavy drinking. It was then ordered that pins or nails would be fastened inside drinking vessels and that whoever drank beyond such a mark in a single draft would be severely punished. This gave rise to the expression "pin-drinking," "to drink to pins" or "nick the pin." **Syn**: pin tankard.

p'ei. A type of beer made in ancient China during the Tang Dynasty (618-907). It was a popular non-filtered beer also called "floating ants" because of the refuse of grains floating at its surface. **See also**: t'ien tsiou; shu; chie; li; sang-lo.

pelletized hops. Synonym for hop pellets.

penny pot. In 17th century England the price of a quart of best ale was one penny while that of small ale was fixed at one halfpence.

pentosan. A hemicellulose present in cereals and other plant tissues. It yields five carbon atom sugars (pentoses).

pentose. Any carbohydrate containing five atoms of carbon.

peptization. The stabilization of colloidal solutions (called SOL) by the addition of electrolytes (peptizing agent) which are adsorbed on the particle surface.

peptonization temperature. The optimum temperature for the degradation of nitrogenous matter during mashing: 45 to 50°C (113 to 122°F).

percent alcohol (by weight or volume). **See**: alcohol by weight; alcohol by volume.

Perle. A variety of hops grown in West Germany containing 7.0 to 8.5% alpha acids and also in Oregon with a 9.0 to 11.0% alpha acids content.

permanent hardness. The hardness of water after boiling. **See also**: water hardness.

perry. A fermented drink like cider, made from pear juice, especially in England.

PET. In England, a plastic container for beer with a capacity of 1.5 liters.

pH. Abbreviation for potential hydrogen, used to express the degree of acidity and alkalinity in an aqueous solution, usually on a scale of 1 to 14, where H$^+$ is the hydrogen-ion concentration. Technically, pH is defined as the negative logarithm of the effective hydrogen-ion concentration in gram equivalents per liter of solution: pH = $\log_{10}$ (1/(H$^+$)). A pH value of 7 (pure water at 25°C) indicates neutrality, one below 7 (7 to 1) indicates acidity and one above 7 (7 to 14) indicates alkalinity. The pH can be measured by specially prepared pH test papers. **Syn:** pH value.

pH measurement. The determination of the hydrogen-ion concentration in an ionized solution.

pH value. Synonym for pH.

phenolic. Describes an unpleasant solvent-, medicinal- or chemical-like flavor. **Syn:** medicinal.

phenols. Volatiles found in small quantities in beer. Higher concentrations, due to the brewing water, infection of the wort by bacteria or wild yeasts, cleaning agents or crown and can linings, impart off-flavors described as phenolic, medicinal or pharmaceutical. Sixty volatile phenolic compounds are present in beer and their concentration is greater in dark beers than in pale beers.

Phorodon humuli. Scientific name of the Damson-hop aphid.

piece. In traditional floor malting, a couch or layer of germinating barley usually about 10 cm (four inches) thick. In pneumatic malting each piece or bed of barley in the germination box is about three feet deep. **See also:** couching; matted couche; mat plow; turner; thinning the piece.

Pils. Synonyn for Pilsener.

Pilsen. Synonym for Pilsener in Germany.

Pilsener. A general name for pale, golden-hued, highly hopped bottom-fermented beers. The original Pilsner was first brewed at the Bürgerlisches Brauhaus in the Bohemian town of Plzeň (meaning green meadow) in Czechoslovakia in 1842. It was then the palest beer available and the style was soon copied worldwide. The archetypal Pilsner is presently known as Plzensky Prazdroj or Pilsner Urquell (Urquell means "original source") and the name was patented in 1898. It is brewed from an original wort gravity of 12°B for an alcohol content of 4% by weight (5% by volume) with very soft, almost mineral-free water. It is highly hopped with local Saaz hops at a rate of 400 to 500 grams per hectoliter (as opposed to 200 to 220 grams per hectoliter for Dormunder). **Syn:** Pils; Pilsner; Pilsen.

Pilsner. Synonym for Pilsener in Czechoslovakia.

pin. A liquid measure of 4.5 imperial gallons (20.45 liters), i.e., half a firkin or one quarter of a kilderkin.

pin tankard. Synonym for peg tankard.

pint. 1. In the United States, a liquid measure equal to 1/8 of a United States gallon, or 29.875 cubic inches (0.473 liter). Also known as liquid pint in distinction of a dry unit of volume of 33.6 cubic inches called pint or dry pint. 2. In England, a dry and liquid measure, also called imperial pint, equivalent to 1/8 of an imperial gallon, or 34.678 cubic inches (0.567 liter). 3. In New South Wales, a beer glass with a capacity of 20 ounces. **See also:** reputed pint.

pinte. An old French capacity measure for liquids equal to half a *quarte* or 0.931 liters.

pitch, to. 1. To spray the inside walls of a cask or barrel with pitch to protect the beer from infection. 2. To pitch with yeast: the action of adding yeast to the cooled wort.

pitch. A black sticky substance derived from coal-tar. It is sprayed into casks and barrels as a protective layer against moisture and infections.

pitcher. A large jug made of metal but more often of earthenware, usually with a handle and spout or lip.

pitching. 1. The addition of yeast to the wort once it has cooled down to a minimum of 24 to 27°C (75 to 80°F). The ideal pitching temperature for top fermenting yeasts is usually 14 to 15°C (57 to 59°F) whereas that for bottom fermenting yeasts is 6 to 8°C (43 to 47°F). **Syn**: yeasting. 2. Coating the inside walls of wooden barrels and casks with pitch or tar to prevent the beer from coming in contact with the wood.

pitching machine. A spraying unit for spraying pitch inside casks and barrels.

pitching rate. The amount of yeast required to ferment a single batch of beer, usually 200 to 600 grams of pressed yeast per hectoliter of wort.

pitchy taste. An off-taste caused by improper pitching of the casks or their having been filled before proper cooling of the pitch.

pito. In Nigeria, a type of beer made from malted sorghum.

piva. An alcoholic beverage prepared in the Aleutian Islands by fermenting potatoes, raisins and other sugar-containing products.

pivo. Czechoslovakian for beer.

piwo. Russian and Polish for beer.

piwowar. Brewer (Polish).

piwowarstwo. Brewery (Polish).

piwsko. Bad beer (Polish).

placbier. The name given to first quality beer (also called bière de luxe) in Belgium in the 15th century.

plaster of Paris. A common name for gypsum.

plate heat-exchanger. A type of heat exchanger consisting of a series of alternating flat and undulated plates.

Plato. A saccharometer expressing the specific gravity as the weight of extract in a one hundred gram solution at a temperature of 17.5°C, 64°F. This percentage is called degree Plato. The original saccharometer was devised by Balling in 1843 but his tables were slightly erroneous and were later corrected by Dr. Plato for the German Imperial Commission (Normal-Eichungskommission). Abbrev: °P. **See also**: Balling; Régie; Belgian degree; specific gravity.

Conversion of Degrees Plato to Degrees Balling							
°P	°B	°P	°B	°P	°B	°P	°B
1	0.97	6	5.92	11	10.9	16	15.95
2	1.95	7	6.90	12	11.90	17	16.95
3	2.92	8	7.90	13	12.90	18	17.95
4	3.91	9	8.90	14	13.94	19	18.95
5	4.91	10	9.90	15	14.95	20	19.97

Plimsoll line. In England, a line on beer glasses to indicate a full measure. Etym: After Samuel Plimsoll. The Plimsoll line (or mark) is the water line of a ship.

plumule. Synonym for acrospire.

pneumatic malting. A method of germinating barley in bulk in thermostatically-controlled and ventilated boxes or drums. It was invented by Dr. Baud at the Tourtel brewery in Tantonville, France. Nicholas Galland patented, also in France, one of the first germination boxes in the 1970s. **See also**: box malting; drum malting; Saladin box.

pocket. A long and large canvas sack containing 50 to 150 kilograms of loose, dry hops.

polish, to. To brush the malt free of dust and other foreign particles.

Polyclar. An insoluble plastic polymer used as a processing aid to prevent chill haze in beer and oxidation browning and pinking in wine.

polyphenol. A complex organic compound partly responsible for chill haze in beer.

polysaccharide. A complex carbohydrate consisting of ten or more monosaccharide units joined together by the expulsion of a water molecule. Includes: starch, cellulose, dextrins.

pombé. 1. Pronounciation: pombay. A beery drink made from millet in Guinea, Africa. It is drunk during ceremonies and purification rites; the alcoholic sensation derived from it is believed to be a sacred means of rejecting disorder in the soul and of attaining a rebirth in serenity. Pombé is prepared by women as follows: after having been steeped, germinated and sun-dried, the red grains of millet (sorghum) are crushed into a flour, mixed with water and gombo stems and simmered in large clay pots for an entire day. The brew is then drawn into a second vessel and boiled overnight. Come morning more flour and water is added, and the day after the brew is again drawn and medicinal or magical herbs are added. Pombé, when ready, is slightly hazy, yellow and foamy, rich in vitamin B and low in alcohol. **Syn**: tan; pombo. **2.**

In Rwanda and Ouganda, a type of beer prepared from banana juice. It is prepared by women from bananas that are neither too ripe nor too green (the first mature too quickly and the second do not contain enough sugars). The bananas are peeled and buried in sand for three days, then they are placed on a cow hide, covered with branches and trampled. The juice is put in pots which are heated; herbs are added for flavoring. The pombé is later drawn in wooden pots which have been rubbed with burnt sorghum flour. A yeasty product is then prepared from sorghum or millet. Fermentation takes 48 hours at as close a constant temperature as possible.

pony. 1. A small liquid measure of one fifth of a pint. 2. In New South Wales, a small five-ounce beer glass. In Victoria and Western Australia, the same term applies to a smaller glass of only four ounces.

Poperinge. A variety of hops from Flanders.

Poperinge Hoppefeesten. A hop festival held every third year in Poperinge, Belgium. The festival begins with a folkloric procession of young hops, children dressed in red and yellow (the colors of the city) and wearing hop-flower-like hats. It is followed by a hop-picking contest and beer drinking festivities.

porridge. A brewer's name for mash. In France it is sometimes called the *salade*.

porter. A very bitter, very dark, almost black and mildly alcoholic top-fermented beer first brewed in Shoreditch, London, in 1730 by a man named Harwood as a substitute for a then popular mix of ale, beer and twopenny called three-heads. It was then called Entire and was advertised as being richer and more nourishing than ale and was intended for porters, carters and other heavy laborers who would find in it the strength to accomplish tasks that no spirit drinker could perform. It was nicknamed porter's ale and, eventually, simply porter. Its dark color was derived from roasted, unmalted barley and sometimes a dash of licorice. In the British Isles, porter was overtaken in popularity by bitter stout in the 19th century and the last porter was brewed in Dublin in 1973. Porter is still brewed today, mostly by bottom fermentation, in East Germany, North and South America, Africa, China, Denmark, Hungary, Poland and Russia. Its alcohol content varies between 5.0 and 7.5% by volume.

Porter Gaff. A cocktail consisting of porter (or stout) and lemonade.

porter's ale. See: porter.

posset. A traditional English drink made from hot milk curdled with ale, wine or other liquor, sweetened with sugar and flavored with spices. There are numerous recipes one of which suggests mixing one liter of hot ale flavored with sugar, powdered ginger and grated nutmeg and one liter of hot milk. **Syn**: ale posset.

pot. In Queensland and Victoria, a beer glass generally of ten-ounce capacity.

In Western Australia the same term applies to glasses of ten-, fifteen- or twenty-ounce capacities.

potable water. Synonym for drinking water.

pot ale. Synonym for spent grains.

potential alcohol. An estimate of the final alcohol content of a beer based on the original gravity or the measured sugar content prior to fermentation.

pothouse. An obsolete name for a low-grade tavern or alehouse. Also spelled: pot-house.

powdery mildew. Synonym for hop mold.

ppm. Abbreviation for parts per million, measurement should be defined as volume or weight.

precipitation. A clarification process that coagulates impurities causing them to sink.

premium. A marketing term used by brewers to qualify the top of their product line.

preservative. A chemical substance added to beer to slow down or prevent oxidation, deterioration or infection.

preservative value. The antiseptic or preservative value of hops as calculated by the formula: $PV = 10(a - a + b - a/3)$. It was found that the preservative value of alpha acids $(a - a)$ was three times as great as that of beta acids $(b - a/3)$. Since the antiseptic potency of alpha and beta acids depends largely upon the pH of the medium and other factors, this formula is not recognized internationally. Abbrev: P.V. or PV.

pressure regulator. A device for controlling the pressure in beer containers.

pressurization. The process of controlling the tightness of casks and kegs by pressurizing them and soaking them in water.

pricking. The natural process by which beer gradually turns sour through the action of acetic organisms on alcohol.

pricked beer. Beer turned sour or that has acquired a vinegar smell and taste.

Pride of Ringwood. A variety of hops grown in Idaho containing 5.5 to 7.0% alpha acids.

prima melior. Beers brewed in medieval monasteries (853 AD) were classed in three categories according to their quality. First quality beer, *prima melior* or *celia*, was served to the fathers and distinguished guests; the second quality, called *secunda* or *cervisia*, was for laymen, and *tertia* or third quality was for travelers and pilgrims. This tradition has survived in some Belgian abbeys where three strengths of beer are brewed classed accordingly as single, double or triple.

primary. Short for primary fermentation bin.

primary attenuation. The attenuation measured at the end of primary fermentation.

primary fermentation. The first stage of fermentation carried out in open containers and lasting from two to seven days during which time the bulk of the fermentable sugars are converted to ethyl alcohol and carbon dioxide gas. **Syn**: principal fermentation; initial fermentation. **See also**: aerobic fermentation.

primary fermentation bin. Synonym for primary fermenter.

primary fermenter. An open vessel in which primary fermentation is carried out. **Syn**: primary fermentor; primary fermentation bin; primary; primary fermentation vessel.

primary fermentor. Orthographic variant for primary fermenter.

priming. The addition of small amounts of fermentable sugars (preferably corn sugar or syrup) to fully fermented beer before bottling to induce a renewed fermentation in the bottle and thus carbonate the beer. **See also**: dry priming; over-priming.

priming sugar. Corn or cane sugar added in small amounts to bulk beer prior to racking or to each bottle prior to capping to induce a new fermentation in the bottle and thus create carbonation. Homebrewers use about 3/4 to one cup of sugar per five-gallon batch of beer.

Primus, Jean. See: Gambrinus.

principal fermentation. Synonym for primary fermentation.

private label beer. Any beer brewed by a local brewer for a private entrepreneur, a large-scale retailer or independent distributor. Examples: Billy Beer (after Billy Carter), Nude Beer and New Amsterdam Amber Beer.

Prohibition. A law instituted by the Eighteenth Amendment (after the Volstead Act) on January 18, 1920, forbidding the sale, production, importation and transportation of alcoholic beverages in the United States of America. It was repealed by the Twenty-first Amendment on December 5, 1933 (at 5.32 P.M.).

Prohibition Bureau. A federal government agency established in 1920 to enforce the National Prohibition Act.

Prohibition-days beer. Beer made during the Prohibition era from odd recipes calling for such ingredients as potato peels, raisins, baker's yeast and others.

Prohibition era. The thirteen years, ten months and eighteen days (January 16, 1920 to December 5, 1933) during which the Eighteenth Amendment was in force.

Prohibition-style beer. In homebrewing, refers to a poor or mediocre beer made by amateurish techniques and low-grade products.

propylene glycol alginate. A foam-stabilizing additive, the modified extract of a seaweed, usually added at a rate of about 160 ppm (0.0160%) in some commercial beers.

protease. A malt enzyme that develops in barley during germination and is capable of degrading complex proteins into polypeptides and amino acids.

protein. An organic compound basically composed of carbon, hydrogen, oxygen, nitrogen and sulfur contained in animal and plant tissues. All proteins are composed of large configurations of twenty amino acids. Proteins are responsible for the head retention and body of beer and partially for its hazyness.

proteinaceous layer. Synonym for aleurone layer.

proteolysis. The hydrolysis of a protein molecule into amino acids by proteolytic enzymes.

proteolytic enzyme. An enzyme that hydrolyzes complex proteins into simpler soluble bodies. **See also:** amylolytic enzyme.

Provisie. A brown beer brewed in Oudenaarde, Belgium. It is aged for a minimum of 2 years and a maximum of 25 years and contains about 6% alcohol by volume.

Pseudoperonospora humuli. Scientific name of downy mildew.

Psylloides attenuata. Scientific name of the hop flea beetle.

P.U. Abbreviation for Pasteurization Unit. Also spelled: PU.

pub. A diminutive for public house.

pubgoer. One who frequents public houses.

public house. In England, an establishment where alcoholic beverages are sold and consumed. Syn: pub.

pull-date. The deadline after which unsold beer should be removed from the shelf and recalled to the company (usually around 60 days).

pulp filter. Synonym for mass filter.

pulque. An alcoholic beverage obtained in Mexico and some parts of Central America by fermenting the juice (called *aguamiel*, honey water) of an agave cactus (genus *Amaryllidaceous*) of the Maguey type, especially Agave atrovirens, A. potatorum, A. americana and A. tequilana. It has an alcoholic content of 6 to 7% alcohol by volume. Tequila and mescal, sometimes called pulque-brandies, are produced by distilling pulque.

pulque curado. Pulque mixed with fruit juices especially pineapple.

puncheon. A large cask varying in size according to commodity: 72 imperial gallons (± 325 liters) for beer, 120 imperial gallons (545 liters) for whisky or brandy, 114 imperial gallons (518 liters) for rum.

punt. The hollow at the bottom of a bottle. **Syn:** kick.

purchase. The name sometimes given to the thumbpiece on a tankard.

Purl. 1. Synonym for Dog's Nose. **2.** A type of mild ale prepared from plant roots, herbs and spices. **3.** Early Purl, a drink consisting of hot ale, wormwood, sugar and gin, was taken in England in the 1800s as a morning appetizer.

purity. Synonym for brilliance.

purity law. See: Reinheitsgebot.

P.V. Abbreviation for preservative value. Also spelled: PV.

pyment. 1. A variety of melomel prepared by fermenting a must of honey, raisin juice and water. **2.** Honey-sweetened wine. Sometimes spelled: pymeat.

quart. A liquid measure. **See also**: U.S. quart; imperial quart.

quarte. An old French measure for liquids with a capacity of 46 cubic inches or 1.863 liters. Also spelled: carte.

quartern. The fourth part of various units of measure.

quas(s). **1.** Orthographic variant for kvas(s).

quiet process. **See**: Burton Union System.

Rr

R. Abbreviation for Régie (° Régie).

rack, to. To transfer beer from one vessel into another or into bottles and casks while leaving the dregs at the bottom of the first container.

racker. An apparatus for racking.

racking. The process of transferring fermented beer from the maturation vat into packaging containers — bottles, cans, casks, kegs.

racking cock. A two-holed nozzle on isobarometric (counterpressure) bottle fillers; it is inserted in the mouth of the bottle to pour the beer while evacuating the air. A third hole creates a counterpressure of air prior to the flow of beer.

racking square. A large holding vessel from which beer is racked-off.

racking tube. In homebrewing, a U-shape tube of rigid plastic with an inlet approximately one and a half inches above the bottom and used with a siphon to draw beer from the fermenter or storage vessel while leaving the dregs behind.

radicle. Root. The lower part of the anis of an embryo seedling; the root part; often the hypocotyl (part of the anis or stem), sometimes together with the root; a rudimentary root. **See also:** rootlets; malted couche.

Radlermass. In Germany, a mix of beer and lemonade. The term means cyclists' beer. **See also:** Russ.

raisonable. In France, a one liter beer glass.

Rauchbier. In Germany, a dark, bottom-fermented beer produced by a few breweries in the city of Bamberg in northern Bavaria. Its unique roasted or smoked flavor results from the use of malts which are dried over an open-fire of moist beechwood logs, a technique dating back, according to some researchers, to 1678. **Syn**: Bamberg beer; Bamberger Rauchbier; smoked beer.

raw sugar. Brown unrefined sugar crystals covered with a film of syrup.

real ale. In England, unpasteurized, cask-conditioned draft ale which completes its maturation in the pub cellar as opposed to pasteurized, filtered and chilled kegged ale. Real ale is served at room temperature, ideally 13.3°C (60°F). Also spelled: Real Ale.

real attenuation. The attenuation of beer devoid of alcohol and carbon dioxide. The carbon dioxide is evaporated and the alcohol is removed by distillation. In the brewing industry only the apparent attenuation is used to measure the progress of fermentation.

Formula: $A = (B-b)/B \times 100$

A = real attenuation

B = original gravity in °B or °P

b = specific gravity of beer devoid of alcohol and CO_2

recrating machine. Synonym for crater.

red mead. A variety of melomel prepared by fermenting a must of honey, red currants and water.

red mold. Synonym for hop mold.

reducing valve. A valve to control the pressure on a fluid, liquid or gas.

Régie. In France, a measure of the density of wort. The legal density is defined as the ratio of the mass of a given volume of liquid (usually 50 cm³) at 15°C to that of the mass of an equal volume of water at 4°C (1 liter of water = 1 kilogram). The *densité Régie* is obtained by moving the comma of the legal density two digits to the right; hence, a legal density of 1,045 = 4.5 degrees Régie (°R). The formula: °R = (Legal density - 1,000) x 100 or (D 15/4 - 1) x 100. One degree Régie equals 2.6 degrees Balling. **See also**: biere.

regulator-carbonator. A type of carbonator used in the carbonated beverage industry to ensure a regulated ratio of carbon dioxide gas and sugar.

Reinheitsgebot. A German law the title of which signifies "pledge of purity" or "order of purity." This purity law governs the production and quality of beer in Germany. Inspired by an earlier law instituted in 1487 by Duke Albert IV, William VI, the Elector of Bavaria, decreed in 1516 that only water, malted barley, malted wheat and hops could be used to make beer. Yeast was not included but taken for granted. This law is still effective today in West Germany and was adopted by some neighboring countries. German law prohibits the use of adjuncts, including sugar, in brewing. A priest also would admonish reinheitsgebot to girls to remain pure-virgins.

Reinheitsgebot-pure. In homebrewing, refers to a beer made from the four basic ingredients; namely, malted barley or malted wheat, water, hops, and yeast without the addition of adjuncts or chemical additives.

repitch, to. To add yeast to induce a renewed fermentation. See also: reyeasting.

reproduction phase. The period following the lag phase during which the yeast cells divide at a constant rate and the cell count doubles at each generation in regular increments of time. The optimal temperature for yeast reproduction is 30°C (86°F); however, this varies dramatically with yeast strain. **Syn:** logarithmic phase; exponential phase.

reputed pint. 1. In Britain, a half bottle (1/12 of an imperial gallon or 0.38 liter). **2.** In South Australia, a beer glass with a capacity of fifteen ounces.

reputed quart. In British measure equal to 1/6 of an imperial gallon (0.75 liter).

residual extract. The residual gravity as determined by evaporating one-third of the volume of the beer, thus eliminating all the alcohol and carbon dioxide, and readjusting the sample to its original gravity with the addition of distilled water.

resin. The gummy organic substance produced by certain plants and trees. Humulone and lupulone for example are bitter resins produced by the hop flower.

resin scum. The brownish substance found on the froth of beer during primary fermentation.

resinification. The oxidation and polymerization of humulone (alpha acid) and lupulone (beta acid) during the storage of hops. The crystalline bitter acids gradually lose aroma, bittering and antiseptic power and are transformed, in the early stages, into soft resins and, eventually, hard resins which are useless to the brewing process. **See also:** soft resins; hard resins.

respiration. The absorption of oxygen and production of carbon dioxide by germinating barley that is caused by the activity of the embryo and the rest of the aleurone. A lack of oxygen during steeping results in the formation of anaerobic substances such as ethanol, lactic acid and esters.

respiratory phase. The second aerobic stage of the fermentation process immediately following the lag period, so-called because the yeast draws oxygen from the wort to oxidize a variety of acid compounds. During this stage, six-carbon sugar (glucose) is first converted into three-carbon acid (pyruvic acid) causing a significant drop in pH; the pyruvic acid is then reduced to activated acetic acid (acetyl CO-A), immediately followed by the Krebs cycle. **See also:** lag period; fermentation phase; Krebs cycle.

rest beer. Unracked beer and sediments at the bottom of a storage tank.

returnable. Is said of packaging material which may be returned, refunded and reused.

re-yeasting. Inducing a secondary fermentation during maturation by adding a little yeast to a brew still containing fermentable sugars but lacking live yeast cells. Also spelled: reyeasting.

rice. Grain of the cereal grass plant *Oryza sativa*. As an adjunct, rice is appreciated for its 70% starch, the highest starch level of any cereal. Its moisture content is around 11 to 13% and it has a low protein level of 7 to 9%. Rice may be added to the mash to increase its starch content and correct an excess of protein. In the United States the addition of 40 to 50% rice is not uncommon while in Europe a ratio of 10 to 20% is more frequent.

rice beer. Synonym for saké.

rice wine. Synonym for saké.

rinsing machine. A machine for rinsing bottles and casks after washing.

roast, to. To expose to fire.

roasted barley. Unmalted barley that has been kilned to a dark brown color similar to that of chocolate or black malt but with a different flavor.

roasted malt. Malt made from barley heated in a sequence of stages starting at 160°C (320°F), then 215°C (419°F) and finally 220 to 225°C (437°F). The malt acquires a brilliant external appearance while the endosperm becomes black. Roasted malt is used to flavor stout and dark beers. **Syn:** Vienna malt.

rocky heads. See: kraeusen.

roller mill. Synonym for grinder.

roquille. An old French (in Paris) capacity measure for liquids equal to 1/32 of a pint.

root beer. A non-alcoholic beverage flavored with oil of wintergreen and oil of sassafras.

rootlets. The seminal roots that grow in a tuft-like formation on germinating barley. **Syn:** malt sprouts. **See also:** culms; coombs; kaulms; radicle, matted couche; couch.

rotary sparger. A hydraulically-operated apparatus fitted in the lauter tun for spraying hot water on the mash. **Syn:** rotary sparget.

round. A name given in the 18th century to vertical cylindrical wooden tuns each holding 300 gallons.

rouser. Synonym for brewer's paddle.

rousing. The action of stirring thoroughly the contents of a vat, tank or cask, usually as an aid to fermentation.

ruh. A term once used to describe the process (or period) of cold secondary fermentation or maturation in bottom-fermented beer.

ruh beer. Bottom-fermented beer ready for lagering.

runchera. See: chicha.

Russ. In Germany, a mix of wheat beer and lemonade. **See also:** Radlermass.

Russian stout. In Britain, a very strong stout originally brewed, from 1780 to World War I, by the London-based Anchor Brewery (now part of the Courage Corp.) for exportation to St. Petersburg in Russia. Present-day Russian stout, brewed by Courage, is non-pasteurized and matured in casks for two months and afterwards bottle-aged for one full year before it is marketed. It is brewed from an original wort gravity of 1101.8 and contains about 10.5% alcohol by volume. Because of its high gravity and its fruity flavor, Russian stout is more properly called barley wine. **Syn:** Imperial Russian stout; Imperial stout.

rye. Grain from the cereal plant *Secale cereale*.

Ss

Saaz. Pronounciation: tsotz. A variety of hops grown in Bohemia in western Czechoslovakia containing 6.5 to 8.6% alpha acids. It is ideal for flavoring Pilsner-type beers.

saccharase. Synonym for invertase.

saccharification. The natural process through which malt starch is converted into fermentable sugars, mainly maltose.

saccharifying enzyme. Synonym for beta amylase.

saccharometer. A type of hydrometer for measuring the sugar concentration of a solution by determining the specific gravity. The reading shows the percentage extract by weight which is converted into percentage by volume by multiplying the reading by the specific gravity or by finding the equivalent volume in tables computed by Balling and Plato.

Saccharomyces. A genus of the Ascomycetes class of yeasts, subfamily Saccharomycetoideae. All species of this genus have the common property of generating ethyl alcohol from sugar. They are differentiated on the other hand by their ability to ferment the carbohydrates galactose, maltose, sucrose, melibiose, lactose, raffinose and starch. Etym: So named by the German chemist Mayer in 1830 when he first isolated yeast under a microscope. Saccharomyces is a scientific translation of an earlier expression, sugar mushrooms, given to yeast by Schwann. **See also:** zuckerpilz.

Saccharomyces cerevisiae. Scientific name for top-fermenting yeast.

Saccharomyces carlsbergensis. Scientific name for bottom-fermenting yeast.

Saccharomyces uvarum. Scientific name for bottom-fermenting yeast.

saccharose. Synonym for sucrose.

saccharum. A brewer's name for invert sugar.

sack metheglin. Sweet-tasting metheglin.

sage ale. Misnomer for an infusion of sage leaves formerly used (17th century) for medicinal purposes.

sahti. A type of homemade beer brewed in Finland from a mix of barley and rye malts, flavored with hops and juniper berries and partially clarified with straw and branches. Sahti may contain up to 10% alcohol by weight.

Saint Arnold(us). See: Saint Arnou.

Saint Arnou. The patron saint of brewers, born in 580 in the Chateau of Lay-Saint-Christophe in the old French diocese of Toul, north of Nancy. He married Doda with whom he had many sons, two of whom were to become famous: Clodulphe, later called Saint Cloud, became bishop of Metz (658-696), and Anchise who married Begga, daughter of Pépin de Landen and mother of Charlemagne. St. Arnou was acclaimed bishop of Metz in 612, a role he assumed for fifteen years and ten days after which he asked Dagobert permission to retire to a monastery near Remiront where he died on August 16, 640. In 641 the citizens of Metz requested that the body be exhumed from Saint Mont and ceremoniously carried to Metz where he was to be buried in the Church of the Holy Apostles. It was during this voyage that a miracle took place in a town called Champigneulles. The tired porters and followers stopped for a rest and a drink. Regretfully there was only one mug of beer to be shared, but that mug never went dry and filled everyone's mug. Also spelled: Saint Arnoul(d); Saint Arnold(us); and sometimes Saint Arnou le Lorrain in distinction of Saint Arnou de Oudenaarde.

Saint Bartholomew. Patron saint of mead; his birthday is celebrated on August 23.

Saint Margaret's ale. A misnomer for water.

saison. An amber- or copper-colored top-fermented beer from Walloon Belgium and France once brewed in the summertime (April-May) from a high gravity wort and drunk four to six months later but now available all year round. Saison is naturally conditioned in burgundy-shaped one liter bottles. It has a fruity flavor and an alcohol content of about 4.5% alcohol by weight (5.6% by volume).

sakazuki. A small porcelain bowl for drinking saké.

saké. A traditional Japanese fermented drink made from rice. Contrary to popular belief, saké is not a spirit (it is not distilled) nor is it a wine (it is not macerated) but rather a special type of beer brewed from a cereal base. The rice is washed, steamed and fermented with a yeast-like fungus (*Aspergillus orgyzae*) which acts both as a saccharifier and fermenter. Primary fermentation takes from 30 to 40 days, after which more rice and water is added to generate a secondary fermentation lasting 8 to 10 days. A special yeast, Saccharomyces saké, is sometimes added to activate fermentation. The alcohol content varies between 14 to 17% by volume. Saké is colorless, slightly hazy, lacks carbonation and is served warm (±37.8°C, 100°F). Etym: From Osaka, Japan. **Syn:** (Japanese) rice wine; (Japanese) rice beer. Also spelled: sake. **See also**: amasaké; shirosaké; shoto saké; sakazuki; tokkori.

Saladin box. A pneumatic germination system invented by Jules Alphonse Saladin in France in the 1880s. The term is now synonymous with germination box.

salt. 1. Common name for sodium chloride, table salt. **2.** Any compound produced by the reaction of an acid with an alkali. Example: calcium chloride.

saltwater. Synonym for brine. Also spelled: salt-water.

salty. An undesirable taste in beer caused by salt.

sang-lo. A type of rice beer made in China during the Tang Dynasty (618-907) and later. Sang-lo was a regional beer produced in the southern region of Su-chou.

saturate, to. 1. Synonym for to carbonate. **2.** To carbonate a liquid to its limit capacity.

saturation. 1. Synonym for carbonation. **2.** Carbonation to the limit capacity of a liquid under specific conditions of temperature, pressure and sugar content. Water for example can dissolve 6.8 grams/liter of CO_2 at 10°C and 2 kg/cm² of pressure. Most beers contain between 4.5 and 5.0 grams/liter of CO_2.

saturator. Synonym for carbonator.

Savinja Goldings. A variety of hops grown in Yugoslavia containing 6 to 7% alpha acids.

Schankbier. In Germany, the weakest category of beers prepared from wort gravities of 7.0 to 8.0°B and containing 2 to 3% alcohol by weight. **See also**: Starkbier; Vollbier; Bier.

schechar. Orthographic variant for shekar.

Schnelle. A very tall, slender tankard of stone- or earthenware with a slightly tapering body and a cover fitted with a thumbpiece.

schooner. 1. A tall beer glass with a capacity of fifteen ounces. **2.** In South Australia the same term applies to a glass of only nine ounces.

Schulties Berliner Weisse. See: Berliner Weisse.

Scotch ale. A top-fermented beer of Scottish origin but now also produced in Belgium and France with an alcohol content of 7 or 8% by volume. Scotch ales are traditionally strong, very dark, thick and creamy. One particular example is brewed by Peter Maxwell Stuart in his castle at Traquair (20 miles south of Edinburgh) and available on location from May to September. In Scotland, the pub expression for such a beer is "wee heavy," which also is the brand name of such an ale produced by Fowler.

screw cap. A type of beer bottle stopper to be twisted on or off rather than pried off like crown corks.

screw stopper. A type of sealing stopper first introduced in 1885 now largely superseded by crown corks.

scum. The white froth that forms at the surface of the primary fermentation vessel.

scurvy grass ale. 1. A medicinal drink formerly prepared by adding an infusion of watercress to ale. It was believed to guard against scurvy. **2.** An infusion of watercress.

scutellum. The shield-shaped sheet of tissue (cotyledon) separating the embryo of the barley grain from the endosperm.

sealed bottle. A bottle hermetically capped.

secondary. Synonym for secondary fermenter.

secondary attenuation. The attenuation measured at the end of secondary fermentation.

secondary fermentation. 1. The second, slower stage of fermentation carried out in closed containers at 4 to 8°C (39 to 46°F) for top-fermenting beers and at 0 to 2°C (32 to 36°F) for bottom-fermenting beers and lasting from a few weeks to many months depending on the type of beer. **See also**: anaerobic fermentation. **2.** A renewed fermentation in bottles or casks engendered by priming or re-yeasting.

secondary fermentation bin. Synonym for secondary fermenter.

secondary fermenter. Any closed container in which secondary fermentation is allowed to occur. **Syn**: secondary fermentation bin; secondary fermentor; secondary.

secondary fermentor. Orthographic variant for secondary fermenter.

second running. Synonym for second wort.

second wort. The wort obtained by sparging the spent grains. **Syn**: second running; spargings. **See also**: first wort.

sediments. The refuse of solid matter that accumulates at the bottom of fermenters and conditioning vessels. **Syn**: settlings.

Seidel. A large German beer tankard with a capacity exceeding one pint.

sekkar. Orthographic variant of shekar.

sérieux. In France, a beer glass for the "serious" drinker with a capacity of two liters.

set mash. A condition that occurs during lautering when the wort is drained too quickly and a bed (fine powder mixed with grain husks) collapses and packs into a tight mass preventing the flow of the wort. **Syn:** stuck mash; dead mash.

settlings. Synonym for sediments.

settling tub. A vessel in which fermentation is first started in commercial breweries.

Shandy (Gaff). 1. Originally, a drink made of beer and ginger, ginger beer or ginger ale. 2. A mix of beer and lemonade, sometimes called Lemon Shandy. **See also:** panaché; Radlermass; Russ.

shekar. 1. A Hebrew word meaning to be or to become inebriated. (Isaiah, 5,11). 2. A beery drink made from corn, dates and honey and drunk by Sem, Noah's eldest son. Also spelled: shecar; sekkar; schechar.

shelf life. The length of time that a bottle or can of beer can be left on a shelf before spoiling. A pasteurized beer has a greater life expectancy than an unpasteurized one; the same is true of dark beers versus pale beers, of beers of high alcoholic content as opposed to lighter ones, and of heavily hopped beers over milder ones. Beers kept cold also survive longer. Unpasteurized draft beer should be drunk within 30 days at the most while pasteurized bottled or canned beer may be stored up to 60 days. Additives are often used to prolong the shelf life of packaged beer. **Syn:** beer life; life expectancy. **See also:** pull-date.

shimeyane. An alcoholic beverage produced in South Africa by fermenting brown sugar, brown bread and malted corn.

shirosaké. A weak, colorless saké (± 5% alcohol by volume).

shive. 1. A circular wooden bung for casks. 2. A small hole pierced in the wooden bung (or shive) of a cask into which the publican or cellarman inserts a wooden peg to control the escape of gas. **Syn:** spile.

Shot and a beer. A small glass of liquor chased with a tall glass of beer.

shoto saké. A Japanese drink made by fermenting sugarcane juice.

shu. A type of millet beer made in China during the Han Dynasty (200 BC) at the beginning of the Chinese Empire. **See also:** li; chiu; t'ien tsiou; pei; sang-lo.

sicera. A strong hopped drink (*Cicera ex lupulis confectam*) made by the Jews during their captivity in Babylon. It was believed to immunize against leprosy.

sieve, to. In malting, to separate grains according to size by means of a sieve having apertures of known size. **Syn:** to bolt.

sight glass. A glass apparatus placed at the exit end of a filter to judge the limpidity of the fluid.

sikaru. The name given to "grain wine" on Mesopotamian clay tablets (ca 8000 to 4000 BC) found during the archeological excavations at Sumer. Sumeria once stretched between two rivers, the Tigris and the Euphrate, in what is Iraq today. Sikaru was made by steeping a bread made from malted barley in water for three to four days and was drunk with a straw or reed. The brewery was called Bit Sikari and the brewer Pa-e-bi. The ale-houses were managed by women called Tsabitu. The goddess of beer was named Nin-Bi, and Siris, daughter of Ninkasi, was the goddess of wort. Sixteen varieties of beer were produced in both pale and dark colors; eight were made from spelt (an early form of wheat), five from barley and three from a mix of spelt and barley. Sikaru was flavored with spices especially cinnamon. The same term was later used in Babylonia as late as 562 BC. **See also:** bi-se-bar.

Sike's hydrometer. A hydrometer invented in 1816 by Bartholomew Sike, a British excise officer, for measuring the alcoholic strength of beverages, especially spirits, giving readings from 70 over proof to zero.

silica gel. A hard, amorphous, granular form of hydrated silica used to adsorb nitrogen matter in beer.

single-stage fermentation. In homebrewing, complete fermentation carried out in a single container that is fitted with a fermentation lock as opposed to two-stage fermentation that first takes place in an open primary fermenter and later in a closed secondary fermenter.

single-stage fermenter. In homebrewing, a wide-mouthed container made of food-grade plastic and fitted with an airtight cover and removable cap for inserting a fermentation lock, usually with a capacity of 7 or 8 United States gallons (5.8 to 6.7 imperial gallons).

siphon. In homebrewing, clear plastic tubing four to six feet long with an inside diameter of about 3/8 of an inch used to draw beer from one container to another.

siphon clamp. A spring device made of steel or plastic (nylon) used in homebrewing to crimp the siphon and thus easily start and stop the drawing process.

six-rowed barley. A variety of barley having three rows of fertile spikelets at each node on which six rows of grains are ultimately formed. Because it has a thicker husk and a less well developed grain than two-rowed barley it yields less extract. Scientific name: *Hordeum hexastichum.* **Syn**: six-row barley; winter barley.

skim, to. To remove the froth or scum that forms at the top of the fermentation vat.

skimming. 1. Removing the scum on the surface of the first head of the fermenting brew. 2. Recovering the top-fermenting yeast at the surface of the wort prior to pouring off. **See also:** crop.

skimming oar. An instrument used to remove the yeast at the surface of the fermentation vessel. **See also:** parachute.

skimmings. The floating dust, light corns and awns at the surface of the steeping liquor.

skirt. The wavy contour of a crown cork that is pressed around the mouth of the bottle.

small ale. An obsolete term once used in England to describe an ale of low alcoholic strength.

small beer. 1. In early England, a weak beer probably made from the washings of the mash as opposed to strong beer which was made from the first running. In 14th century England, small beer sold for 1 penny and was called penny ale, whereas the stronger version was known as better beer. **2.** In early America, a beer of low alcohol content for daily consumption. George Washington had a recipe for "small beer." **3.** In Queensland, Australia, a five-ounce beer glass. **4.** Generally speaking, a weak or diluted beer.

smoked beer. See: Rauchbier.

smooth. Giving a pleasant sensation.

Society for the Preservation of Beers from the Wood. A British association of beer enthusiasts which, in 1973, gave rise to the Campaign for Real Ale (CAMRA).

soft resins. One of the two fractions secreted by the lupulin gland during the development of the hop cones. Soft resins are composed mainly of about 45% alpha acids (alpha resins or humulones) and 25% beta acids (beta resins or lupulones). Extracted from hops during the boiling stage, they contribute most of the 900 bittering substances in beer. The alpha acids are substantially isomerized to iso-alpha-acids while some of the beta acids are oxidized to bitter materials such as hulupones. **Syn:** bitter resins. **See also:** hop oils; hard resins.

soft water. Water devoid of calcium and magnesium salts.

SOL. Abbreviation for colloidal solution (one that flows), a liquid in which are suspended solid particles of colloidal dimensions. **See also:** gel.

sor. Hungarian for beer.

sora. A beer made from maize in Peru prior to the arrival of the Conquistadores. It was apparently much stronger than chicha and was not available to the common mojica.

sorghum. A cereal grain from various grasses (*Sorghum vulgare*), also known as kaffir corn in South Africa where a sorghum beer is produced.

sorghum beer. Synonym for kaffir beer.

soubya. Egyptian rice beer.

sour. Taste perceived on the sides of one's tongue as with lemon juice.

souring. The spoiling of beer caused by bacteria contamination.

sparge, to. To spray hot water on the spent grains after mashing.

sparging. In mashing, an operation consisting in spraying the spent grains in the mash with hot water to retrieve the liquid malt sugar remaining in the grain husks. To prevent the mash from packing, the sparging volume of water must equal the volume of wort coming out at the base of the mash tun thus maintaining a constant level. Also, by maintaining the level of hot water above the filter-bed, the oxidation of the tannin in the husks is reduced considerably. **See also**: set mash; lautering.

spargings. Synonym for second wort.

sparging water. The fine spray of hot water used for sparging, the temperature of which must be the same as that of the mashing liquor.

sparkle, to. To foam or bubble.

sparklet cartridge. A non-refillable CO_2 cartridge used with pressurized beer kegs to maintain a constant pressure while the keg is emptied.

sparkling. Effervescence caused by fermentation.

sparkling ale. In Adelaide, Australia, a top-fermented beer similar to Britain's pale ale. A U.S. term for a class of ales brewed mostly before Prohibition to compete with lagers.

sparkling mead. A mead made effervescent by a secondary fermentation in the bottle.

Spaten water. Water from the artesian wells of the Spaten brewery in Münich. An analysis of those waters, among the most famous in the world, conducted in 1880, gave the following composition in grams per liter: carbonate of lime 0.12, carbonate of magnesia 0.077, sodium carbonate 0.057, potassium sulfate 0.009, lime sulfate 0.003, sodium nitrate 0.019, silica 0.014, iron and aluminum oxides 0.001, organic matters 0.022 and sodium chloride. **See also**: brewing water.

special beer. Any beer produced by spontaneous fermentation. Example: gueuze, lambic, faro.

special bitter. Bitter ale prepared from an original wort gravity of 1.049 to 1.055. It is maltier and sweeter than best bitter. **Syn**: strong bitter. **See also**: bitter.

specific gravity. A measure of the density of a liquid or solid as compared to that of water which, by convention, is given the value 1.000 at 4°C (39.2°F). For the sake of accuracy, the specific gravity of liquids should always be measured as closely as possible to that temperature. The specific gravity is a dimensionless quantity (with no accompanying units) because it is expressed as a ratio in which all dimensions cancel. Abbrev: S.G.; s.g.

spelt. 1. A primitive species of wheat, the grains of which do not thresh free of the chaff. **2.** *Triticum spelta*, an intermediate between wheat and barley grown to some extent in Germany and Switzerland. A local name for emmer (*triticum dicoccum*)—a wheat species having a spike broken up into segments and grains that do not thresh free of chaff. They are tetraploid wheats. Also spelled: speltz.

spent grains. The refuse of grain husks remaining in the mash tun after lautering. They contain about 25% protein and are useful as a nitrogenous addition to cattle fodder. **Syn:** draff; brewers' grains.

spent hops. The refuse of hops remaining after the boiling process. They are compounded with ferrous sulfate and other mineral salts and used as artificial horticultural fertilizers.

Spezyme. A group of four enzymes, Spezyme BBA, Spezyme AA, Spezyme GA (glucoamylase) and Spezyme IGI (immobilized glucose isomerase) developed by Powell & Scholefield laboratories in England and manufactured by the Finnsugar Group, a Finland sugar corporation. Spezyme BBA, a beta amylase extracted from barley, is used in the brewing industry to standardize or raise the diastatic power of diastatic malt extracts. Spezyme AA, an endoamylase derived from a selected strain of *Bacillus subtilis*, readily hydrolyzes gelatinized starch into soluble dextrins. It is used in the traditional cooking process of whole grains when an additional beta-glucanase activity is desired. Spezyme GA, a glucoamylase, is used in the brewing industry to produce low carbohydrate beer. **See also:** Supavit Z.

.Sphaerotheca mucalaris. Scientific name for hop mold.

spigot. 1. A device for regulating the flow of beer from a cask or barrel. **2.** A tap for a cask.

spile. 1. The hole atop of a beer cask. **2.** Synonym for shive.

spitzmalt. German for pointed malt, a hard malt made from barley that has barely germinated.

split. Synonym for nip.

spreader. An apparatus that spreads out the flow of malted barley evenly over the mill rollers.

spring barley. Barley, sown in spring.

spruce beer. 1. Traditionally, a beery beverage produced in North America and Northern Europe by fermenting molasses and other sugars with the exudate of spruce trees or a decoction of the buds and cones of such trees, sometimes with malt. **2.** Danzig spruce beer: a black beer produced in Danzig by fermenting the sap and young shoots of the black spruce tree (*Picea nigra*) with a sugary wort of molasses or maple sugar. **Syn**: black beer.

stacking. The action of piling casks one tier above the other.

stale ale. In 16th century England, the name given to one year-old ale.

stale flavor. Synonym for off-flavor.

stale yeast. A yeast containing dead cells resulting in a slow starting fermentation or no fermentation at all.

starch. Formula: $C_6H_{10}O_5$. Any of a group of carbohydrates or polysaccharides secreted in the form of granules by certain cereals, composed of about one-quarter amylose (inner shell) and three-quarter amylopectin (outer shell). Starch hydrolyzes to yield dextrins and maltose through the action of amylases. Barley starch is enclosed in the endosperm and constitutes 63 to 65% of the weight of two-rowed barley and about 58% of that of six-rowed barley. **See also**: amylose; amylopectin.

starch test. A simple test to ascertain if all the malt starch has been converted to maltose. It consists in adding a drop of tincture of iodine to a drop of cold wort on a clean white saucer. If the color remains iodine-brown the starch conversion is complete, whereas a blue or purplish blue coloration is indicative of the presence of starch and that mashing must continue. Since iodine is toxic, the test sample must not be returned to the mash. **Syn**: iodine test; iodine starch test.

Starkbier. In Germany, one of the three legal categories for beers comprising those brewed from an original gravity of at least 16°B and containing no less than 5% alcohol by weight. **See also**: Bier; Schankbier; Vollbier.

starter. A separate batch of fermenting yeast to be added to the bitter wort once it has cooled down to 21°C (70°F). In homebrewing, it is prepared by pitching yeast in a quart of wort cooled to about 24°C (75°F), preferably one or two days in advance. The yeast starts to activate and multiply while the bulk of the wort undergoes cooling. When the wort has reached room temperature the starter is roused and added to the wort and stirred again.

starting gravity. Synonym for original gravity.

starting specific gravity. Synonym for original gravity.

stave. Each of the thin, curved pieces of wood which, when assembled, constitute a cask or barrel.

stavewood. Synonym for caskwood.

steam beer. A beer produced by hybrid fermentation using bottom yeast fermented at top yeast temperatures (15 to 20°C, 60 to 70°F). Fermentation is carried out in long, shallow pan-like vessels called clarifiers followed by warm-conditioning at 10 to 12°C (50 to 55°F) and kraeusening. This style of beer is indigenous to America and was first produced in California at the end of the 19th century (during the Gold Rush) where temperatures were too warm for proper fermentation of bottom yeasts. At one time there were as many as 27 breweries making steam beer in San Francisco. It is presently brewed by the Anchor Steam Brewing Company under the registered trade-name of Steam Beer, a highly hopped, amber-colored, foamy beer containing 3.8% alcohol by weight (4.74% by volume). Etym: Named after the hissing sound produced by the pressure released when a cask is tapped.

steam heater. An apparatus that produces warm or hot air.

steep, to. To soak barley in water for 40 to 120 hours during which time it acquires humidity and oxygen required for the embryo to germinate.

steep. Synonym for steeping tank.

steeping. The action of soaking hard dry barley in water in a steeping tank for approximately 40 to 80 hours and sometimes up to 120 hours under controlled conditions of temperature (13 to 15°C, 55 to 59°F), humidity (from 10 to 15% to 45 to 50%) and oxygenation, in order to soften them. Steeping is best carried out in stages separated by air rests. A typical steeping schedule would be 12 hours at 15°C (59°F), 12 hours air rest followed by another 16-hour steep. Barley is considered to be sufficiently steeped when the moisture content has reached 42 to 44%. Sometimes called: wetting. **See also:** oversteeping.

steeping tank. A cylindro-conical tank for steeping barley. **Syn:** steeping vat; steep tank; steep.

steeping copper. A large closed vessel in which the wort undergoes boiling and saccharification.

steeping vat. Synonym for steeping tank.

steep liquor. The chalky, alkaline water used for steeping.

steep tank. Synonym for steeping tank.

Stein. A German earthenware drinking vessel with a capacity, in Münich, of 50 centiliters, 1 liter or 3 liters.

steinie. In France, a one liter family-size bottle for beverages such as cider, lemonade and beer.

stemware. A generic term for drinking glasses comprising a stem. Contrary to barware, stemware in used exclusively at the dining table. There are five different glasses: goblet, wine, sherbet or Champagne, cocktail, and cordial.

sterilant. Synonym for sterilizing agent.

sterile. Free of living organisms, especially microorganisms — bacteria, molds and yeasts.

sterilizer. An apparatus for sterilizing objects by means of dry heat, steam or boiling water.

sterile beer. Ultra-filtered beer from which all living organisms, including yeast, have been removed or destroyed.

sterilizing agent. Any substance that will kill all forms of microbial life, including bacteria and other infective organisms, on or inside an object. Homebrewers can prepare a sterilant by one of two methods: **1.** adding two teaspoons of potassium or sodium sulfite (metabisulfite) to one quart of water. A pinch of citric acid helps to activate the release of the sulfur dioxide; **2.** adding two teaspoons of household chlorine bleach to half a gallon (two quarts) of water. In both cases the sterilant must be thoroughly rinsed out with hot water after use. **Syn:** sterilant.

Stiftsbräu. **See:** abbey beer.

stillion. An X-shaped cradle, similar to a saw-horse, on which wooden casks and barrels are rested during maturation to prevent separation of the staves under pressure.

stingo. A strong ale or beer.

stirring spoon. Synonym for brewer's paddle.

stirrup cup. A drinking vessel or cup similar in shape to a rhyton. Such a cup was given to a man mounted on a horse upon his departure or arrival from a long journey. It is often shaped like the head of a hound, fox or fish or like a clenched fist.

stock ale (or beer). An ale brewed very strong to be stored for a long period of time.

stone ale. An ale once brewed at the monastery of Stone in Staffordshire.

stopper. A general name for any type of closing or capping device for bottles and casks. Bottle caps are classed in three main categories based on the type of closure: crown corks, screw stoppers and wire-on stoppers.

stoppered. Fitted with a stopper.

storage. Synonym for secondary fermentation or maturation.

storage cellar. A refrigerated room, originally a cellar, where beer is stored while undergoing secondary fermentation.

storage tank. A vessel or tank in which beer is stored prior to racking.

stout. In Britain, a very dark and very heavy top-fermented beer made from pale malt and 7 to 10% roasted, unmalted barley, often with the addition of caramel malt or sugar. Stout was first introduced by Guinness as an Extra Stout (higher gravity) version of their Plain Porter. The new stout was darker, richer, hoppier and more alcoholic than porter which it gradually overtook in popularity until porter disappeared completely. Today, a distinction is drawn between sweet and dry stout. Although both are highly hopped (600 to 700 grams per hectoliter), sweet stout is less bitter than the dry version. Their alcohol content is about 5% by volume. Etym: Probably from stout ale or stout porter. **Syn:** bitter stout. **See also:** Russian stout; dry stout; sweet stout; porter.

strain, to. To pump or pour a solution through a permeable material to remove solid matter.

strainer. Synonym for hop back.

straining. The action of passing a solution through a screen to separate solid matter from the liquid. In homebrewing a nylon sieve, a muslin bag or a nylon mesh straining bag are used.

strength. 1. The alcohol content of a beer. **2.** The specific gravity of the wort prior to fermentation. **3.** The degree of bitterness of a beer.

stinking water. See: waipiro.

strike temperature. The ideal temperature for a mash rest.

strobile. The flower or cone of the hop plant. **Syn**: hop cone; hop flower.

strong beer. Full strength beer as opposed to small beer.

strong bitter. Synonym for special bitter.

stubbie. A type of beer bottle once popular in the United States of America but now practically obsolete.

stuck fermentation. Fermentation that has stopped prematurely, i.e., before the final gravity has been reached. In homebrewing, this phenomenon may be caused by a weak starter, the destruction of yeast cells by unwashed sterilant, wort that is too hot, or fermentation temperatures that are too low.

stuck mash. Synonym for set mash.

Styrian Goldings. A variety of hops grown in Yugoslavia containing 6.0 to 8.0% alpha acids.

Submarino. A variant of the drink called Depth Charge prepared in Mexico by immersing a shot glass full of tequila in a glass of beer.

substrate. A chemical substance upon which an enzyme acts. The suffix -ase denotes an enzyme which acts upon a particular substrate, i.e., invertase inverts sucrose, maltase hydrolyzes maltose and lactase hydrolyzes lactose. Some enzymes, however, have been known for so long that their original name has been retained, e.g., pepsin.

Sucellus. The god of brewing and coopering in ancient Gaul. He is represented alongside the goddess of mead with a pitcher in one hand and a mallet in the other.

sucrase. Synonym for invertase.

sucrose. A double sugar obtained from sugarcane and sugarbeet. It is not directly fermentable by yeast and must first be hydrolyzed to glucose and fructose by the enzyme invertase secreted by the yeast. **Syn**: cane sugar; beet sugar; table sugar; household sugar; saccharose.

Süddeutsches Weizenbier. Synonym for Weizenbier.

suds. Slang for beer. Etym: from the German word *sud* meaning to brew. German brewers introduced the word into American jargon in the late nineteenth century, where suds became associated with the foam of beer. Suds then became associated with the foam of soap and the use of the term soap suds became popular. During prohibition suds came into general use as a humorous, though somewhat derogatory, reference to beer. Suds factory, a brewery.

sugar. 1. A generic name for a class of carbohydrates including fructose, glucose, maltose, and lactose. 2. Without qualification it invariably refers to sucrose.

sugarbeet. A beet, *Beta vulgaris*, cultivated for its high sugar content (15 to 20%). Also spelled: sugar beet.

sugarcane. A tall stout grass, *Saccharum officinarum*, grown in warm climates and cultivated extensively for its high sugar content which, among its other uses, is a rich source of fermentable sugar. Also spelled: sugar cane.

sugaring. Adding sugar to the wort to increase its sugar content and, consequently, the alcoholic strength of the resulting beer.

sulfuring. Treating with sulfur dioxide.

sun flavor. An off-taste in beer caused by exposure of the beer to sun or light rays. **Syn:** sunstruck.

sunstruck. Synonym for sun flavor or lightstruck.

Supavit Z. A yeast nutrient developed by the Powell & Scholefield laboratories in England, the result of research work into the action of zinc ions on the fermentation of wort by yeast. It is used in the brewing industry to correct any zinc deficiency in the wort while at the same time providing the vitamins, amino acids and trace elements essential to counteract sluggish fermentation.

sweet. Possessing a taste of sugar, the opposite of dry.

sweet mead. A sweet-tasting mead, containing a certain amount of unfermented sugars, as opposed to dry mead.

sweet stout. The English version of stout as opposed to the dry stout of Ireland. It has a slightly lactic flavor and is less alcoholic than dry stout. Sweet stout is typified by Mackeson. **Syn:** milk stout. **See also:** stout.

sweet wort. The sugary liquid obtained by mashing and sparging malt.

swimmer. Synonym for attemperator.

swing stopper. Synonym for wired-on stopper.

table sugar. Synonym for sucrose.

takju. A type of rice beer brewed in Korea. Also spelled: yakju.

Talisman. A variety of hops grown in Washington containing 7.5 to 9.0% alpha acids and about 4.5% beta acids.

talla. A type of beer produced in Ethiopia by fermenting roasted barley, millet or maize and flavored with the twigs and leaves of a local tree. Talla (or dalla) also was prepared in Abyssinia from barley and dagussa (*Pennisetum spicatum*). Barley grains were buried between leaves in a trench of dry soil for three days, unearthed and fashioned into a broad, flat cake called bekel which would later be diluted with water and added to a mix of ground barley and mascilla (white sorghum) to induce fermentation. The mixture was again diluted, boiled and fermented for about ten days. It was flavored, prior to fermentation, with powdered giscio (geshu) leaves.

tan. Synonym for pombé.

Tango. In France, a mix of pale beer and grenadine syrup.

tank. A large storage vessel or container for holding liquids.

tankard. A tall drinking jug on a flat or short molded base with a hinged or removable cover and a single handle used for drinking beer in northern Europe since the Middle Ages.

tannic. Synonym for astringent.

tannic acid. Synonym for tannin.

tannin. Any of a group of organic compounds contained in certain cereal grains and other plants. Hop tannins have the ability to help in the precipitation of haze-forming protein materials during the boiling (hot break) and cooling (cold break) of the wort. Tannin is mainly present in the bracts and stigs of the hop cone and imparts an astringent taste to beer. Also called hop tannin as opposed to tannins originating from malted barley. The greater part of the tannin content of the wort is derived from malt husks, but malt tannins differ chemically from hop tannins. Non-technical term used for phenols. **Syn:** tannic acid. **See also:** phenols.

Tanzemann. A Swiss drinking vessel made of sculptured wood depicting a peasant (which forms the stem) with a basket (which forms the bowl) on his (or her) back. The same vessel is called Buttenmann in Germany.

tap, to. 1. To place a tap in the opening of a cask or keg. **2.** To draw beer from a cask or keg.

tap. 1. A device for regulating the flow of liquids from a keg or cask. **2.** On tap: draft beer.

tap water. Synonym for drinking water.

tapioca. Cassava starch produced by the tuberous roots of the cassava or manioc plant. It is rarely used as an adjunct because its starch has an alkaline reaction that impairs the quality of beer.

taproom. A room in a tavern where draft beer is served.

taste test. A test carried out in industry to evaluate a new product or changes in an existing product, usually held by a panel of experts and consumers.

tavern. 1. Historically, a place where wine was sold as opposed to an ale-house which served beer. **2.** Today, a drinking establishment where until recently only beer was served and only men were allowed. **See also:** brasserie.

tavern-keeper. The owner or licensee of a tavern.

taverner. The owner of a tavern. In early England taverns were owned by vintners who were allowed to sell wine only. In 1635 a law was passed allowing them to also sell ale, beer, food and tobacco. **Syn:** tavern-keeper.

TCA cycle. Abbreviation for tricarboxylic acid cycle, a synonym for citric acid cycle.

TCW. Abbreviation for thousand-corn weight.

temporary hardness. A form of hardness in water caused by the presence of soluble bicarbonates of calcium and magnesium. Temporary hardness, contrary to permanent hardness, is removable by boiling to precipitate the carbonates.

terminal gravity. Synonym for final specific gravity.

tertiary fermentation. Renewed fermentation carried out in bottles for the purpose of conditioning.

testing jar. Synonym for hydrometer jar.

test tube. Synonym for hydrometer jar.

Tettnanger. A variety of hops grown in the Lake Constance region in West Germany containing 7.0 to 8.0% alpha acids and also grown in Idaho, Washington and Oregon containing 4.0 to 6.5% alpha acids and 4.5 to 6.5% beta acids.

texture. Synonym for body.

thermometer. A device for measuring temperature. Thermometers specifically designed for brewers (and winemakers) are normally calibrated from -10 to 110°C (14 to 230°F). They are filled with alcohol rather than mercury so that if they break they will not contaminate the beer (the broken glass can be recuperated through a filter). In homebrewing, a cheese or milk thermometer with a scale ranging from 32°F to 212°F is adequate. **See also:** Centigrade; Fahrenheit.

thin. Is said of a beer lacking fullness of palate or body.

thinning the piece. In traditional floor malting, reducing the thickness of the germinating barley to control the temperature by allowing a greater amount of heat to escape. **See also:** piece.

thousand-corn weight. The average weight of 1,000 (and sometimes 5,000) corns of barley as determined on a dry weight basis, usually around 35 to 45 grams. The greater the weight the higher the extract yield.

Two-rowed barley: $\%E = 84.5 - 0.75 \, P + 0.1 \, G$
Six-rowed barley: $\%E = 80.0 - 0.75 \, P + 0.1 \, G$
$\%E$ = percentage of extract
P = percentage of protein
G = 1000 corn weight in grams.

The protein content of barley varies from 8 to 16% but maltsters usually prefer samples containing 9 to 11%. Abbrev: TCW.

three-heads. In England, a mix of beer, ale and twopenny. It was the precursor of porter.

three-point-two beer. In America, beer not exceeding 3.2% alcohol by volume. Also spelled: 3.2 beer. **See also:** Cullen Act.

thumbpiece. The projecting knob attached to the hinged lid of a covered vessel (flagon or tankard) which, when pressed with the thumb, holds the lid open for drinking. Also spelled: thumb-piece. **Syn:** billet; lever. **See also:** purchase.

Thunaeus test. A laboratory test to determine the germinative capacity of barley by immersing the grains in 0.75 to 1.0% (w/v) hydrogen peroxide. The percent number of grains to have chitted after three days are counted. Non-germinated grains are peeled and encouraged to germinate in wet sand or wet filter pads. The total number of grains to have germinated after both treatments constitute the germinative energy.

tied house. In England, a system by which a pub or inn is tied to a single brewery by mutual agreement.

t'ien tsiou. The name given to millet beer in Chinese texts dating back to 2000 BC. T'ien tsiou is green beer not yet clarified and not fully fermented while Tsiou is a fully fermented and clarified beer. **See also:** shu; li; chiu.

tileque. See: kuchasu.

tiswin. A beer-like beverage once made from corn, wheat, jimson and water by the Apache Indians. Its production was outlawed by the government in 1885. Jimson weed is a *poisonous* annual weed of the nightshade family. Tiswin was made as follows: dry corn, after soaking overnight, was laid on yucca leaves spread over holes in the ground and covered with gunnysack. It was sprinkled with water daily for about one week until germination was complete and the sprouts had grown two inches long. The corn was then spread in the sun to partially dry and later ground and mixed into a dough weighing about 10 pounds. About four gallons of water were then added to the dough, which was boiled in an earthenware vessel to about half its original content after which jimson weeds were added. Lost water was replaced and the mixture boiled again until reduced by half. After straining, ground wheat was added and the liquid was fermented overnight to be drunk the following morning. **Syn:** tulipai (meaning yellow water); oafka.

toasted malt. Pale malt kilned for 10 to 15 minutes at 176.6°C (350°F) producing a toasted aroma to beer.

tokkori. In Japan, a bottle for warming saké.

Tomboy. A mixed drink prepared in a highball glass (8 ounces) by adding half a cup of chilled tomato juice to half a cup of cold beer.

top fermentation. One of the two basic fermentation methods characterized by the fact that dead yeast cells rise to the surface during fermentation. Primary fermentation occurs at 15 to 25°C (59 to 77°F) and lasts for about one week.

top fermentation yeast. Synonym for top-fermenting yeast.

top-fermented beer. Synonym for ale.

total hardness. The sum of temporary and permanent hardness.

top fermenting ale yeast. Synonym for top-fermenting yeast.

top-fermenting yeast. One of the two varieties of brewers' yeast, so called becauses it rises to the surface of the wort during fermentation. It cannot ferment below 13°C (55°F) and works best at temperatures of 15 to 25°C (59 to 77°F). The maximum growth temperature for Saccharomyces cerevisiae is 37.5 to 39.8°C (99.5 to 106.6°F). Compared to bottom-fermenting yeast, ale yeast ferments more rapidly, it has a higher alcohol tolerance but, on the other hand, it does not convert dextrins as well which means that it yields sweeter beers. **Syn:** Saccharomyces cerevisiae; ale yeast; top yeast; top-fermentation yeast; top-fermenting ale yeast.

topping-up. In homebrewer's parlance, adding water after primary fermentation to fill the secondary fermenter, thus reducing the surface area exposed to oxygen.

topuy. A rice beer brewed in the Philippines.

top yeast. Synonym for top-fermenting yeast.

Trappist beer. Any beer brewed in one of the six remaining brewing abbeys, five of which are in Belgium and one in The Netherlands. Trappist beers are top-fermented, deep-hued (amber or brown) and fairly strong, ranging from 5.7 to 12% alcohol by volume (4.6 to 9.6% w/v); they are fruity and often bittersweet; they are bottle-conditioned by priming and re-yeasting. The origin of Trappist beers dates back to the Middle Ages when epidemics were spread by contaminated water. Monasteries located on the travelling route to pilgrimage areas provided travellers with food, shelter and a hygenic beverage free of pathologic microbes. There were many abbeys all over Europe; Germany alone accounted for close to 500. In Belgium, two orders brewed beer: the Benedictines and the Cistercians. After the Revolution, only the Trappists (Cistercians of strict observance) continued to brew beer. There are five brewing abbeys left in Belgium: **1.** Chimay (also known as Abbaye de Notre-Dame-de-Scourmont) located near the French border in the Hainaut Province was founded in 1850. The brewery, built in 1863, produces three distinct qualities distinguished by the color of the bottle caps: Red Cap, White Cap and Blue Cap. Red cap, an amber-colored beer with a thick, dense foam, averages 6 to 6.2% alcohol by volume (4.8 to 5.0% w/v). It is also sold in tall bottles (*bouteilles bordelaises*) sealed with Champagne corks. White Cap is slightly stronger with an alcohol content of 7.55% by volume (6% w/v). Blue Cap is stronger yet, with 8.75% alcohol by volume (7% w/v); it is vintage-dated and reaches peak maturity after two years. **2.** Orval (also known as Villiers-devant-Orval) is situated in the Luxembourg Province near the French border. It was founded in 1070 by Benedictine monks from Calabre who were replaced in the 12th century by monks from Trèves. The present abbey was constructed from 1926 to 1948, and the brewery was built in 1931. It produces a well hopped amber-colored beer of 5.7% alcohol by volume (4.5% w/v). **3.** Rochefort, the Abbaye Notre Dame de St. Rémy, is located near Dinant in the province of Namur. It is closed to the public and the production is limited (20 to 25 hectoliters/year). Three qualities are produced, 6°, 8° and 10° Belgian, the last being the darkest. **4.** St. Sixtus, the Abbaye de St. Sixte, located at Westvleteren in the province of West Flanders, was established in 1831. Their production is limited (3000 hectoliters/year) and their beers are sold on the premises only. Three qualities are produced: 10°, 20° and 25° Balling (6.2, 8.0 and 10.5 to 11.0° Belgian) called Abt, Extra and Special. St. Sixtus beers also are produced commercially by the Brasserie Saint Bernard in Watou of which Prior 8° is the best known. **5.** Westmalle. The abbeys brewery, Notre Dame du Sacré-Coeur, located in the Antwerp Province, was established in 1836. It produces three beers: a Tripple (or Trippel), a golden-hued, creamy beer of 8% alcohol by volume (6.4% w/v): a Double (or Dubbel), darker, sweeter and less alcoholic containing 6% alcohol by volume (4.8% w/v); and a Simple drunk by the monks themselves and not available commercially. Other Belgian monastic orders such as Affligem, Tangerloo, Maredsous and Lesse no longer brew their own beer but have licensed commercial breweries to do so. In The Netherlands, the Trappist abbey of Our Lady of Koningshoven, located near Tilburg in North Brabant, operates a brewery called Schaapskooi (or Skaapskoi, meaning sheep den) in conjunction, originally, with Artois but now with Skol. The fathers brew two beers, a bottom-fermented Pilsener-style brew and a top-fermented Trappist of 6.5% alcohol by volume (5% w/v). **See also:** abbey beer.

tricarboxylic acid cycle. Synonym for citric acid cycle.

trojniack. A slightly sweet mead made in Poland by fermenting a must of one part honey and two parts water with a special strain of Malaga yeast. It averages 12.5% alcohol by volume and is aged for three years. Also spelled: trojniak.

trub. Pronounciation: troob. Suspended particles caused by the precipitation of proteins, hop oils and tannins during the boiling and cooling stages of the wort. **See also:** hot break; cold break; tannin.

tsabitu. The name given to ale wives in ancient Sumeria. **See also:** sikaru.

tsiou. See: t'ien tsiou.

tub. A large open vessel for holding liquids, originally made of wood but now made of metal or plastic.

tulipai. A synonym for tiswin meaning yellow water.

tun. 1. A large vessel for holding liquids. 2. A measure of capacity for holding liquids, 250 wine gallons.

tunnel pasteurization. A method of pasteurization for bottled and canned beer. It consists of a tunnel-like apparatus in which the bottles are sprayed with hot water (pre-heating and pasteurizing (20 min. at 60°C)) and later with cold water (pre-cooling and cooling). The entire process takes about an hour and the output ranges from 2,000 to 60,000 bottles (or cans) per hour. **See also:** flash pasteurization.

tun room. The part of a brewery where fermentation takes place.

tuplak. In Czechoslovakia, a boot-shaped glass used on festive occasions and at beer-drinking contests.

tuppenny. Synonym for two-penny.

turbidity. Cloudiness in a beer. **See also:** haze; chill haze.

turner. A tool for turning the malt and separating matted rootlets. Syn: malt oar; malt turning device. **See also:** couche; malted couche; malt plow.

Twenty-first Amendment. See: Prohibition.

two-penny. A pale, small beer sold in England in the 18th century at 4 pennies per quart or 2 pennies per pint. Also spelled and pronounced: tuppenny or twopenny.

two-rowed barley. A variety of barley on which only the central spikelet in each triad is fertile, forming two rows of grains each. It is the variety most appreciated for brewing because its corn is better developed and the husk is thinner. Scientific name: *Hordeum distichum.* **Syn**: two-row barley; spring barley; Chevalier barley.

two-stage fermentation. Fermentation carried out in two containers, an open vessel for aerobic primary fermentation and a closed vessel for anaerobic secondary fermentation as opposed to single-stage fermentation. **Syn**: double-stage fermentation.

tyg. A communal drinking vessel made of pottery (slipware) with four to six handles, used at convivial gatherings.

Uu

ullage, to. 1. To calculate the headspace (airspace) in a cask or barrel. **2.** To refill a cask or bottle.

ullage. 1. The empty space at the top of a bottle, cask or barrel between the liquid and the top of the container. In standard-size bottles, the headspace is usually one to one and a half inches. Homebrewed beers require up to two inches; an extra volume of air will accelerate oxidation and cause air-breathing bacteria to sour the beer. **Syn**: headspace; airspace. **2.** The amount of liquid that a container lacks of being completely full. It is measured in terms of the volume of liquid required to fill the container to capacity. **3.** The dregs (or liquid) left in a cask after leakage or racking.

ullaged. Is said of a container short of its full measure.

underback. A vessel placed underneath the mashing tun and into which the mash is poured.

under-carbonated. Is said of a beer lacking carbonation or effervescence. In homebrewing this is easily remedied by adding more priming sugar.

underletting. The process of heating the mash by introducing hot water through the bottom of the mash tun.

unhopped. Synonym for non-hopped.

union. See: Burton Union System.

unload, to. To remove the steeped barley from the steeping tank.

under-modified. Malt of high amylase strength containing large amounts of unconverted protein because the germinating barley has been dried and kilned before the proteinase enzymes were totally converted to protein materials.

under-oxygenated. Said of an under-saturated wort, i.e., one containing less than 9 ppm of oxygen, in which the yeast reproduces with difficulty.

unpitching. The action of removing old pitch from inside a cask or barrel. **Syn:** depitching.

Ur-. A German prefix, an abbreviated form of Urtyp meaning original type, used to denote a beer brewed according to the original style.

U.S. gallon. See: gallon

U.K. gallon. Synonym for imperial gallon. **See also:** gallon.

U.S. quart. A capacity measure of 57.75 cubic inches (0.9463 of a liter).

vacuum pump. An apparatus consisting of a cylindro-conical vessel through which a flow of air is pumped to remove dust particles on the barley grains.

vase. A hollow vessel used for holding liquids.

vat. A large vessel for holding liquids during fermentation. Often called: tun.

vegetable gelatine. Synonym for agar-agar.

ventilation. Synonym for airing.

vessel. A hollow receptacle for holding liquids.

Vienna. **1.** An amber-colored, bottom-fermented beer originally brewed in Austria where it is now rare and known as Spezial to differentiate it from the classic version. Vienna-style lagers, still brewed in South America and Mexico, are amber-colored, lightly hopped, malty and fairly strong ($\pm$ 4.4% alcohol by weight or 5.5% by volume). **2.** A term often synonymous with Märzen.

Vienna malt. Malt dried at a slightly higher termperature than pale lager malt; however, its main distinction is in the unique germination process used before drying. A beer made with Vienna malt will be deep gold to light brown.

vitamin C. Synonym for ascorbic acid.

volatiles. The volatiles in beer are divided into seven groups: alcohols (higher alcohols or fusel alcohols), esters, carbonyls, organic acids, sulfur compounds, amines and phenols. These volatiles are responsible for most of the flavors found in beer.

Vollbier. One of the three legal categories for beers in Germany comprising those of medium strength brewed from an original gravity of 11 to 14°B and containing 3.5 to 4.5% alcohol by weight. **See also**: Bier; Starkbier; Schankbier.

v/v. Abbreviation for volume per volume as in percentage volume of alcohol per volume of solution. **See also**: alcohol by volume.

waghebaert. A type of strong beer brewed in Brussels in the 15th century.

waipiro. A Maori word meaning "stinking water" used by that people to describe a brew prepared by Captain James Cook at Dusky Sound, New Zealand, in 1773. This beer was made by boiling the small branches of the manuka and the rimu tree (which he describes as spruce and tea plants) for three to four hours and adding molasses and yeast.

wallop. British slang (cockney) for mild beer.

wash beer. Synonym for distiller's beer.

Wassail Bowl. "In 1732 Sir Watkin W. Wynne presented to Jesus College of Oxford the famous silver gilt bowl which had a liquid capacity of ten gallons. The recipe for the Wassail Bowl or 'Swig' made at the college on St. David's Day consisted of half a pound of sugar put into a bowl with one pint of warm beer poured into it. The dispenser was instructed to grate a nutmeg and some ginger into it; to add four glasses of sherry and five additional pints of beer, to stir it well; and then to sweeten according to taste; to cover it and let it stand for two or three hours, after which he was required to put three or four slices of toast into it — and then it is ready to be served. It is also suggested that two or three slices of lemon, and a few lumps of loaf sugar might be rubbed on the peel of a lemon, might well be introduced to improve the punch." Frank A. King, *Beer Has a History*, London/New York, Hutchinson Scientific and Technical Publications, 1947, p. 100.

water hardeners. Mineral elements such as gypsum, Epsom salt, table salt or Burton salts added to soft or neutral water to render it hard.

water hardness. The degree of hardness of water caused by the presence of mineral elements dissolved into it. It is expressed, in metric usage, in parts of calcium carbonate per million parts (ppm) of water; in England, in Clark degrees (= 1 part of $CaCO_3$ per 70,000 parts of water); in France, a degree of hardness is 1 mg of calcium carbonate ($CaCO_3$) per 1,000 liters of water; in Germany it is valued as 1 mg of calcium oxide ($CaCO$) per 1,000 liters of water. The German figure, when multiplied by 17.9, gives parts per million of calcium carbonates. **Syn:** hardness of water. **See also:** permanent hardness; temporary hardness; hard water; soft water; brewing water.

	ppm	Grain per U.S. gallon	°Clark	°French	°German
1 ppm	—	0.0583	0.07	0.1	0.056
1 grain per U.S. gal	17.1497	—	1.2	1.7149	0.958
1°Clark	14.3	0.833	—	1.43	0.8
1°French	10.0	0.583	0.7	—	0.56
1°German	17.9	1.044	1.43	1.78	—

water lock. Synonym for fermentation lock.

water quality. Refers to biological, chemical and mineral content and properties of water. The quality of water has an impact on the quality and taste of a specific beer-type. To this end the modern brewer can adjust, alter or correct the chemical composition of water by adding or subtracting elements or mineral salts to the required optimal standards. Generally speaking, dark beers are made from soft to neutral water while pale beers are made from hard to neutral water. **See also:** water treatment.

water seal. Synonym for fermentation lock.

water sensitivity. See: dormancy.

water treatment. Altering the characteristics and composition of water by mechanical or chemical means. In homebrewing, hard water is softened by boiling for about 20 minutes and racking, and soft water is hardened by the addition of calcium sulfate (gypsum) and magnesium sulfate (Epsom salt). Half a teaspoon of each to every gallon (4.5 liters) is a good recipe.

weeping barrel. A brewer's term for a leaking wooden barrel or cask caused by separation of the staves.

Weissbier. In Germany, a generic term for wheat beers. The term is more often synonymous with Berliner Weisse than with its southern counterpart (Süddeutsches) Weizenbier. Weisse means white but such beers are usually very pale gold with a white foam. They are sometimes referred to as Weisse beer in English literature. Also spelled: Weisse Bier. **See also:** wheat beer; Lager Weisse.

Weizenbier. In Germany, a generic name for top-fermented wheat beers, especially those of the south (mainly Bavaria, München and Baden-Württemberg), sometimes called Süddeutsches Weizenbier to distinguish from those of northern Germany, which are referred to as Berliner Weisse or simply Weissbier. Compared to the northern Berliner Weisse, Weizenbier has a much higher wheat-to-barley ratio (1:1 to 2:1 as opposed to 1:3), a higher density (12 to 14°B as opposed to 7 to 8°B) and a higher alcohol content (+5% by volume as opposed to 3 to 4%). Weizen is also fuller flavored but less acid. It is bottle-conditioned and is available in two forms: with yeast sediments (Weizen mit Hefe or Hefeweizen(bier)) or without (Hefefreiweizen(bier)), both of which are often preferred with a slice of lemon. In Bavaria, wheat beer also is known as Bayerischer Weize. **Syn:** Süddeutsches Weizenbier. **See also:** wheat beer.

Weizenbock. In Germany, a wheat beer of bock strength; i.e., 5.0% by weight (6.25% by volume).

wet kit. A homebrewing kit containing a syrupy concentrate of wort as opposed to a dry kit which contains flour.

wetting. A rare synonym for steeping.

wheat. A cereal from any of the grasses of the genus *Triticum*. There are thousands of varieties, divided into two categories: *Triticum vulgare* (or *Triticum aestivum*) or soft wheat, and *Triticum durum* or hard wheat (also called Durum wheat). **See also:** adjunct.

wheat beer. Any beer containing a high proportion of malted wheat. Such beers are now produced only in Germany and Belgium. Belgian wheat beers include blanche de Hoegaarden, blanche de Louvain and lambic. German wheat beers are classed in two categories: the Weissbier or Berliner Weisse of northern Germany and the Weizenbier or Süddeutsches Weizenbier of southern Germany (mostly Bavaria and Baden-Württemberg). All wheat beers are top-fermented and many are bottle-conditioned by the addition of yeast. The Belgian wheat beers contain 30 to 50% wheat, the Berliner Weisse 25 to 30% and the Bavarian Weizenbier contains 50% or more.

whicked weed. A depreciatory name given to hops by ale-brewers in 15th century England.

whirlpool. An apparatus for the clarification of beer consisting of a large cylindrical tank about as tall as it is broad. The wort is introduced at high speed through a pipe set tangentially at about mid-point in the vertical wall. As the wort comes to rest in the tank, the trub or hot break deposits as a cone at the bottom by a process of sedimentation. The whirlpool often is used in conjunction with a hop separator.

white ale. An medicinal concoction once prepared in Devon and Cornwall by mixing beer and rum with eggs, salt and flour.

white mold. Synonym for hop mold.

Whitsan church ale. Synonym for Whitsun ale.

Whitsontide ale. Synonym for Whitsun ale.

Whistun ale. A church ale and feast in 16th and 17th century England. Also called: Whitsontide ale or Whitsan church ale.

whole hops. Synonym for loose hops.

Wieze Oktoberfesten. A beer festival held annually in Belgium (since 1956) from September 30 to October 15.

wild beer. 1. A beer fermented by wild yeasts. 2. Synonym for gushing beer.

wild yeast. 1. Any airborne yeast. 2. In the fermenting wort, any yeast other than the cultured strain used for fermentation (*Saccharomycae cerevisiae* or *Saccharomycae carlsbergensis*).

Willamettes. An American variety of hops developed to improve the low acreage yield of Fuggles and increase its alpha acid content. It is grown in Oregon with a 5 to 6% alpha acid content.

winter barley. A synonym for barley, sown at the end of autumn.

Witbier. See: Hoegaardse Wit and Leuvense Wit.

withering. Blowing dry air into barley after germination is complete so as to decrease the ratio of humidity in the green malt.

wood alcohol. Synonym for methyl alcohol.

wood chips. Synonym for clarifying chips.

wood strips. Synonym for clarifying chips.

work, to. To ferment.

wort. Pronounciation: wert. The bittersweet sugar solution obtained by mashing the malt and boiling-in the hops before it is fermented into beer. **See also:** sweet wort; bitter wort.

wort boiler. Synonym for brew kettle.

wort chiller. An apparatus used in homebrewing to cool the wort rapidly.

wort copper. Synonym for brew kettle.

wort cooler. Synonym for wort receiver.

wort kettle. Synonym for brew kettle.

wort receiver. A cooling vessel into which the wort is poured after straining the hops. **Syn:** wort cooler.

wort straining. The process of straining the wort through a filter.

w/v. Abbreviation for weight per volume as in percentage weight of alcohol per volume of solution. **See also:** alcohol by volume; alcohol by weight.

Wye Target. A variety of hops grown in England containing 10 to 11% alpha acids.

Xx, Yy

yakju. An orthographic variant for takju.

yard-of-ale. A three-foot-long horn-shaped drinking glass that holds about a quart of beer and consists of a long fluted neck resting on a globular bottom similar in shape to a coach horn. It was originally intended to be drained at a single draught. **Syn:** ale-yard; aleyard; yard-of-beer; long glass.

yeast. Microscopic, unicellular, vegetal organisms of the fungus family (*Eumycophyta*) distinct from bacteria since they possess a true nucleus. Yeasts are classed in one of three categories depending on their ability to sporulate and the method of sporulation: *Ascomycetes, Basidiomycetes,* and *Fungi imperfecti*. Brewing yeast (or brewers' yeast) are classed into three categories: bottom-fermenting yeast or Saccharomyces carlsbergensis, reclassified Saccharomyces uvarum; top-fermenting yeast or Saccharomyces cerevisiae; and wild yeasts such as Saccharomyces candida and other species. Each category is further subdivided into strains. Since yeasts belong to the plant family, they are named according to the International Code of Botanical Nomenclature; each yeast is known by a binomial combination, the first name being that of the genus (or family), the second that of the species. Over 500 types of yeasts have been isolated, not including the numerous wild strains. The rate of reproduction of yeasts in wort varies with the temperature and reaches a maximum at about 30°C (86°F). The reproduction rate of Saccharomyces cerevisiae is greater than that of Saccharomyces uvarum at high temperatures and the opposite holds at lower temperatures. Brewer's yeasts are sensitive to heat and may be killed by exposure to temperatures of 52°C (125.6°F) or above for ten minutes or more. During the fermentation process, yeast converts the natural malt sugars into equal parts of alcohol and carbon dioxide gas. Yeast was first viewed under a microscope in 1680 by the Dutch scientist Antonie van Leeuwenhoek and later, in 1867, Louis Pasteur,

(*Études sur le vin*, 1866, *Études sur la bière*, 1876), discovered that yeast cells lack chlorophyl and that they could develop only in an environment containing both nitrogen and carbon. **See also:** bottom-fermenting yeast; top-fermenting yeast; lag phase; reproduction phase.

yeast back. A large open vessel, usually with a capacity of 80 to 500 hectoliters (1,800 to 11,000 gallons), in which top yeast recovered from the fermentation vessel is stored. **See also:** parachute.

yeast bite. A brewer's term describing a sour, bitter taste in beer.

yeast energizer. A vitamin and mineral supplement for brewing yeast used to accelerate its growth.

yeast food. Synonym for yeast nutrients.

yeast head. The yeast-containing froth at the surface of top fermenting ale at the end of primary fermentation. It is sometimes recovered by skimming or suction to be used for pitching further worts.

yeasting. Synonym for pitching.

yeast nutrients. 1. The elements essential to the life and growth of yeast cells which include oxygen, carbon, nitrogen, phosphorus, sulfur, various minerals and certain vitamins, all of which are normally present in aerated wort. Carbon is obtained from glucose, galactose, fructose, sucrose, maltose, maltotriose, maltulose and maltotriulose; nitrogen is obtained from ammonium salts, amino acids and small peptides; phosphorus is obtained from phosphates; sulfur comes from inorganic sulfate or sulfite, thiosulfate, methionine or glutothione. **2.** An additional dose of proteinous compounds and phosphates to ensure that the yeast remains healthy throughout fermentation. If the wort contains less than 60% malt or consists of malt extract, additional nutrients may be required. **Syn:** yeast food.

yellow water. Apache meaning of the word tulipai, a synonym for tiswin.

yield of extract. The percentage of extractable dry matter in the grist; i.e., the total amount of dry matter that passes into solution in the wort during mashing.

Yorkshire stone square. An open fermentation vessel of 36 hectoliters (28 barrels) capacity unique to the town of Tadcaster in Yorkshire. It was originally made of stone and later of slate and consists of two separate sections divided by a deck. The wort is fermented in the main (lower) compartment and the yeast rises over the deck through a manhole that has a 5-inch (15 cm) flange. The beer drains back through pipes while the yeast settles and is skimmed off.

Zz

zitos. The modern Greek name for beer. **See also:** zythos.

zithum. Orthographic variant for zythum.

zuckerpilz. An early name, meaning sugar-fungus, given to yeast by Kützing and Schwann around 1837.

zur. Synonym for kiesiel.

zymase. A complex of enzymes in yeast that are responsible for alcoholic fermentation by converting glucose to alcohol and carbon dioxide gas. Etym: So-named by Eduard Buchner in 1897.

zymology. The science or study of fermentation. **Syn:** zymurgy.

zymometer. An instrument for measuring the degree of fermentation.

zymosis. Fermentation.

zymotechnics. **1.** Synonym for zymurgy. **2.** The science of producing and controlling fermentation.

zymurgy. **1.** Synonym for zymology. **2.** The title of a magazine published by the American Homebrewers Association.

zythos. The Greek name for barley wine, from the Egyptian word zythum.

zythum. An old name for barley wine (beer) made in Pharaoh's Egypt in the Nile Delta. A third-century BC papyrus describes the making of barley wine as follows: six-row barley is mixed with water and baked into a bread which is afterwards broken, crushed and diluted in date juice and water. This is followed by crude filtration and fermentation. It was flavored with juniper berries, powdered ginger, hops, black cumin, safron and other herbs. Dizythum is said to have been a more potent drink, carmi was a palace variety and busa was the familial beer. Also spelled: zithum; zythem.

zymurgy. Also, the last word in *this* dictionary!

Thermometer Scales

The two most commonly used temperature scales in brewing and malting are the traditional Fahrenheit (°F) scale and the metric Centigrade (°C) scale. These scales are based on the freezing and boiling point of pure water.

Freezing point: 0°C   32°F
Boiling point: 100°C   212°F

The Interpolation Factor chart below represents the difference between the nominal starting points 0 and 32 (0°C = 32°F). Each 1°C = 1.8°F and each 1°F = 0.56°C.

Conversion Formulas

°F = (°C x 9/5) + 32   or   (°C x 1.8) + 32
°C = (°F - 32) x 5/9   or   (°F - 32) / 1.8

Interpolation Factors

°C	F/C	°F
0.56	1	1.8
1.11	2	3.6
1.67	3	5.4
2.22	4	7.2
2.78	5	9.0
3.33	6	10.8
3.89	7	12.6
4.44	8	14.4
5.00	9	16.2
5.56	10	18.0

The center column refers to the given temperature in either scale, °F or °C, with the Fahrenheit equivalent on the right and the Centigrade equivalent on the left. Example: 3°F = 1.67°C and 3°C = 5.4°F.

The Temperature Conversion Table on the opposite page uses the same format as above for easy reference.

Temperature Conversion Table

°C	F/C	°F	°C	F/C	°F
0.00	32	89.6	271.11	520	968
4.44	40	104	276.67	530	986
10.00	50	122	282.22	540	1004
15.56	60	140	287.78	550	1022
21.11	70	158	293.33	560	1040
26.67	80	176	298.89	570	1058
32.22	90	194	304.44	580	1076
37.78	100	212	310.00	590	1094
43.33	110	230	315.56	600	1112
48.89	120	248	321.11	610	1130
54.44	130	266	326.67	620	1148
60.00	140	284	332.22	630	1166
65.56	150	302	337.78	640	1184
71.11	160	320	343.33	650	1202
76.67	170	338	348.89	660	1220
82.22	180	356	354.44	670	1238
87.78	190	374	360.00	680	1256
93.33	200	392	365.56	690	1274
98.89	210	410	371.11	700	1292
104.44	220	428	376.67	710	1310
110.00	230	446	382.22	720	1328
115.56	240	464	387.78	730	1346
121.11	250	482	393.33	740	1364
126.67	260	500	398.89	750	1382
132.22	270	518	404.44	760	1400
137.78	280	536	410.00	770	1418
143.33	290	554	415.56	780	1436
148.89	300	572	421.11	790	1454
154.44	310	590	426.67	800	1472
160.00	320	608	432.22	810	1490
165.56	330	626	437.78	820	1508
171.11	340	644	443.33	830	1526
176.67	350	662	448.89	840	1544
182.22	360	380	454.44	850	1562
187.78	370	698	460.00	860	1580
193.33	380	716	465.56	870	1598
198.89	390	734	471.11	880	1616
204.44	400	752	476.67	890	1634
210.00	410	770	482.22	900	1652
215.56	420	788	487.78	910	1670
221.11	430	806	493.33	920	1688
226.67	440	824	498.89	930	1706
232.22	450	842	504.44	940	1724
237.78	460	860	510.00	950	1742
243.33	470	878	515.56	960	1760
248.89	480	896	521.11	970	1778
254.44	490	914	526.67	980	1796
260.00	500	932	532.22	990	1796
265.56	510	950	537.78	1000	1832

Table of Conversion Factors

To convert:	To:	Multiply by:
British barrels	British gallons	36.0
	cubic feet	5.779568
	cubic meters	0.1636591
	liters	163.6546
	U.S. barrels (liq.)	1.3725
British firkins	British pints	72.0
	British gallons	9.0
	cubic centimeters	40,914.79
	cubic feet	1.444892
	U.S. firkins	1.2000949
	liters	40.91364
British gallons	British barrels	0.027777
	British firkins	0.111111
	British ounces (fl.)	160.0
	British quarts	4.0
	cubic centimeters	4,546.087
	cubic feet	0.160544
	cubic inches	277.4193
	cubic meters	0.004546
	liters	4.54596
	U.S. ounces (fl.)	153.7215
	U.S. gallons (liq.)	1.20095
British gal./second	cubic centimeters/second	4.546.087
British ounces (fl.)	cubic centimeters	28.41305
	cubic inches	1.733387
	British gallons	0.00625
	milliliters	28.41225
	U.S. ounces (fl.)	0.9607594
British pints	British gallons	0.125
	British gills	4.0
	British ounces (fl.)	20.0
	British quarts	0.5
	cubic centimeters	568.26092
	liters	0.568245
	U.S. gills	4.903797
	U.S. pints (liq.)	1.200949

To convert:	To:	Multiply by:
British quarts	British gallons	0.25
	cubic centimeters	1,136.522
	cubic inches	69.35482
	liters	1.13649
	U.S. gallons	0.032056
	U.S. quarts (liq.)	1.200949
Centigrade (°C)	Fahrenheit (°F)	(°C x 9/5) + 32
Centigrams	grains	0.15432
	grams	0.01
Centiliters	cubic centimeters	10.0
	cubic inches	0.6102545
	liters	0.01
	U.S. ounces (fl.)	0.33815
Centimeters	feet	0.03281
	inches	0.3937
	meters	0.01
	microns	10,000.0
	millimeters	10.0
Centimeters/minute	inches/minute	0.3937
Centimeters/second	feet/minute	1.969
	feet/second	0.03281
	meters/minute	0.6
	meters/second	0.01
Cubic centimeters	British gallons	0.000218997
	British gills	0.007.39
	British quarts	0.00087988
	British ounces (fl.)	0.03519
	cubic feet	0.000035314
	cubic inches	0.06102
	cubic millimeters	1,000.0
	liters	0.001
	milliliters	1.0
	U.S. drams (fl.)	0.27051
	U.S. gallons (liq.)	0.00026417
	U.S. gills	0.0084535
	U.S. ounces (fl.)	0.033814
	U.S. pints (liq.)	0.00211337

Table of Conversion Factors

To convert:	To:	Multiply by:
Cubic centimeters	U.S. quarts (liq.)	0.0010567
Cubic feet	British gallons	6.229
	British ounces (fl.)	996.6143
	cubic centimeters	28,316.847
	cubic meters	0.028317
	cubic inches	1,728.0
	liters	28.31685
	U.S. gallons (liq.)	7.481
	U.S. pints (liq.)	59.844256
	U.S. quarts (liq.)	29.922078
	U.S. ounces (fl.)	957.50649
Cubic inches	British barrels	0.000797
	British gallons	0.0036
	cubic centimeters	16.38706
	cubic feet	0.00058
	cubic meters	0.0000163
	cubic millimeters	16,387.06
	liters	0.01639
	U.S. gallons	0.004329
	U.S. pints (liq.)	0.034632
	U.S. quarts (liq.)	0.017316
	U.S. ounces (fl.)	0.554
Cubic meters	British barrels (liq.)	6.11
	British gallons	219.9692
	cubic feet	35.3147
	cubic inches	61,023.74
	liters	1,000.0
	U.S. barrels (liq.)	8.3864145
	U.S. gallons (liq.)	264.17205
	U.S. pints (liq.)	2,113.3764
	U.S. quarts (liq.)	1,056.6882
	U.S. quarts	1,056.688
	liters	1,000.0
Cubic millimeters	Cubic inches	0.000061
Drams (avoirdupois)	grains	27.3437
	grams	1.7718
	drams (apothecaries)	0.455729
Drams (apothecary)	Drams avoirdupois	0.2.194286

To convert:	To:	Multiply by:
Drams (apothecary)	pounds avoirdupois	0.008571429
	pounds troy	0.010416667
	ounces troy	0.125
	ounces avoirdupois	0.1371429
	pennyweight	2.50
Fahrenheit (°F)	centigrade (°C)	(°F x 5/9) - 32
Feet	centimeters	30.48
	inches	12.0
	meters	0.3048
	millimeters	304.8
	mils	12,000.0
Feet/minute	centimeters/second	0.508
	meters/second	0.00508
	meters/minute	0.305
	m.p.h.	0.011364
Feet/second	centimeters/second	30.48
	meters/minute	18.288
	meters/second	0.3048
Firkins	*See U.S. firkins and British firkins.*	
Gallons	*See U.S. gallons and British gallons.*	
Grains avoirdupois	Grains troy	1.0
Grains troy	grains avoirdupois	1.0
	drams (apothecaries)	0.01666
	drams (avoirdupois)	0.03657
	grams	0.0647989
	milligrams	64.7989
	ounces apothecaries	0.002083
	ounces avoirdupois	0.0022857
	ounces troy	0.002083
	pennyweight	0.0416667
	pounds avoirdupois	0.0001428
	pounds troy	0.0001736
	scruples	0.05
Grams	decigrams	10.0
	drams avoirdupois	0.5643

Table of Conversion Factors

To convert:	To:	Multiply by:
Grams	drams apothecary	0.2572
	grains	15.43235
	kilograms	0.001
	milligrams	1,000.0
	ounces avoirdupois	0.03527
	ounces troy	0.03215
	pennyweight	0.64301
	pounds avoirdupois	0.00204
	pounds troy	0.002679
	scruples	0.77162
Hectoliters	cubic feet	3.531566
	liters	100.0
	U.S. gallons (liq.)	26.41794
	U.S. ounces (fl.)	3,381.497
Hundredweight (long)	kilograms	50.80235
Hundredweight (short)	kilograms	45.35924
Imperial (measures)	*See British (measures)*	
Inches	centimeters	2.54
	feet	0.083333
	meters	0.0254
	microns	25,400.0
	millimeters	25.4
	mils	1,000.0
Kilograms	British gallons	0.2199
	British quarters (long)	0.078736522
	cubic centimeters	1,000.0
	cubic inches	61.023
	drams avoirdupois	564.4
	grains	15,432.358
	grams	1,000.0
	hundredweight (long)	0.01968
	hundredweight (short)	0.02204
	ounces avoirdupois	35.2739
	ounces troy	32.15074
	pounds avoirdupois	2.20462
	pounds troy	2.6792
	pennyweight	643.015
	scruples	771.61792

To convert:	To:	Multiply by:
Kilograms	tons (long)	0.009842
	tons (metric)	0.001
	tons (short)	0.0011023
	U.S. gallons	0.26417
Kilometers	feet	3,280.84
	yards	1,093.6133
Liters	British gallons	0.21997
	British gills	7.03902
	British ounces (fl.)	35.196
	British pints	1.795756
	British quarts	0.8798775
	centiliters	100.0
	cubic centimeters	1,000.0
	cubic feet	0.03532
	cubic inches	61.0255
	cubic meters	0.001
	drams (fl.)	270.5179
	milliliters	1,000.0
	U.S. gallons (liq.)	0.26417205
	U.S. gills	8.4535058
	U.S. ounces (fl.)	33.8147
	U.S. pints (liq.)	2.1133764
	U.S. quarts (liq.)	1.0567
Liters/minute	cubic feet/minute	0.0353147
	cubic feet/second	0.000588578
Liters/second	cubic feet/minute	2.11888
	U.S. gallons (liq.)/minute	15.850342
	U.S. gallons (liq.)/second	0.2641723
Meters	centimeters	100.0
	feet	3.28084
	inches	39.37008
	kilometers	0.001
	millimeters	1,000.0
Meters/second	feet/second	3.281
	feet/minute	196.86
Microinches	microns	0.0254
Microns (micrometer)	centimeters	0.0001

Table of Conversion Factors

To convert:	To:	Multiply by:
Microns (micrometer)	inches	0.000039
	microinches	39.37008
	millimeters	0.001
	mils	0.03937
Milligrams	centigrams	0.1
	drams apothecaries	0.0002572
	drams avoirdupois	0.000564
	grains	0.015432
	grams	0.001
	ounces avoirdupois	0.00003527
	ounces apothecaries	0.00003215
	pennyweight	0.000643
	scruples	0.0007716
Milliliters	British ounces (fl.)	0.035196
	British pints	0.001759804
	cubic centimeters	1.0
	cubic inches	0.06102
	cubic milliliters	1,000.0
	liters	0.001
	U.S. drams (fl.)	0.2705198
	U.S. gills	0.008453742
	U.S. ounces (fl.)	0.0338149
	U.S. pints (liq.)	0.002113436
Millimeters	centimeters	0.1
	cubic centimeters	1.000028
	cubic inches	0.061025
	feet	0.00328
	inches	0.03937
	meters	0.001
	microns	1,000.0
	mils	39.37
Mils	centimeters	0.00254
	inches	0.001
	microns	25.4
	millimeters	0.0254
Ounces (fl.)	*See U.S. ounces (fl.) and British ounces (fl.).*	
Ounces avoirdupois	Centigrams	2,834.9527
	cubic centimeters	28.35

To convert:	To:	Multiply by:
Ounces avoirdupois	cubic inches	1.73
	drams (avoirdupois)	16.0
	grains	437.5
	grams	28.3495
	kilograms	0.02835
	ounces troy	0.911458
	pennyweight	18.22917
	pounds avoirdupois	0.0625
	pounds troy	0.07595
	scruples	21.871
Ounces troy	centigrams	3,110.3481
	drams avoirdupois	17.5543
	drams apothecaries	8.0
	grains	480.0
	grams	31.103481
	kilograms	0.03110348
	ounces avoirdupois	1.09714
	milligrams	31,103.481
	pennyweight	20.0
	pounds avoirdupois	0.06837
	pounds troy	0.08333
	scruples	24.0
Parts per million	Grains per U.S. gallon	0.0584
	grams per U.S. gallon	0.0038
	grams per liter	0.001
	ounces per barrel	0.0042
	milligrams per liter	1.0
Pints	*See U.S. pints and British pints.*	
Pounds avoirdupois	British quarts	0.399
	cubic centimeters	453.59
	cubic feet	0.016
	drams avoirdupois	256.0
	grains	7,000.0
	grams	453.5924
	kilograms	0.4535924
	ounces avoirdupois	16.0
	ounces troy	14.5833
	pennyweight	291.667
	pounds troy	1.21528
	scruples	350.0
	U.S. quarts (fl.)	0.4793

Table of Conversion Factors

To convert:	To:	Multiply by:
Pounds troy	drams apothecaries	96.0
	drams avoirdupois	210.65
	grains	5,760.0
	grams	373.24177
	kilograms	0.3732417
	ounces apothecaries	12.0
	ounces avoirdupois	13.1657
	ounces troy	12.0
	pennyweight	240.0
	pounds avoirdupois	0.822857
	scruples	288.0
Quarts	*See U.S. quarts and British quarts.*	
Revolutions/minute	revolutions/second	0.01667
Revolutions/second	revolutions/minute	60.0
Scruples	drams apothecaries	0.33333
	drams avoirdupois	0.73142
	grains	20.0
	grams	1.29597
	ounces apothecaries	0.04166
	ounces avoirdupois	0.0457
	ounces troy	0.04166
	pennyweight	0.8333
	pounds apothecaries	0.003472
	pounds avoirdupois	0.002857
	pounds troy	0.003472
Square centimeters	square feet	0.001076
	square inches	0.155
	square meters	0.0001
	square millimeters	100.0
	square mils	155,000.31
Square feet	square centimeters	929.03
	square inches	144.0
	square meters	0.0929
Square inches	square centimeters	6.4516
	square feet	0.00694
	square meters	0.000645
	square millimeters	645.16

To convert:	To:	Multiply by:
Square meters	square centimeters	10,000.0
	square feet	10.7639
	square inches	1,550.0
Square millimeters	square centimeters	0.01
	square feet	0.00001
	square inches	0.00155
Tons (long)	kilograms	1,016.047
	ounces avoirdupois	35,840.0
	pounds apothecaries	2,722.22
	pounds avoirdupois	2,240.0
	pounds troy	2,722.22
	tons (metric)	1.01605
	tons (short)	1.12
Tons (metric)	kilograms	1,000.0
	ounces avoirdupois	35,273.96
	pounds apothecaries	2,679.2289
	pounds avoirdupois	2,204.6226
	pounds troy	2,679.2289
	tons (long)	0.9842
	tons (short)	1.10231
Tons (short)	kilograms	907.185
	ounces avoirdupois	32,000.0
	pounds apothecaries	2,430.555
	pounds avoirdupois	2,000.0
	pounds troy	2,430.555
	tons (long)	0.89286
	tons (metric)	0.90718
U.S. firkins	British firkins	0.8326747
	cubic feet	1.203125
	liters	34.06775
	U.S. barrels	0.29464286
	U.S. pints (liq.)	72.0
U.S. gallons (liq.)	British gallons	0.83267
	cubic centimeters	3,785.412
	cubic feet	0.13368
	cubic inches	231.0
	cubic meters	0.003785
	liters	3.7854
	U.S. ounces (fl.)	128.0

Table of Conversion Factors

To convert:	To:	Multiply by:
U.S. gallons (liq.)	U.S. pints (liq.)	8.0
	U.S. quarts	4.0
U.S. gallons/hour	liters/hour	3.7854118
U.S. gallons/second	cubic centimeter/second	3,785.4118
	cubic feet/minute	8.020833
	liters/minute	227.1183
U.S. ounces (fl.)	British ounces (fl.)	1.040843
	cubic centimeter	29.57373
	cubic inches	1.8046875
	liters	0.0295727
	U.S. gallons (liq.)	0.0078125
	U.S. gills	0.25
	U.S. pints (liq.)	0.0625
	U.S. quarts (liq.)	0.03125
U.S. pints (liq.)	British pints	0.8326747
	cubic centimeters	473.17647
	cubic feet	0.01671
	cubic inches	28.875
	liters	0.4731632
	milliliters	473.1632
	U.S. gallons (liq.)	0.125
	U.S. ounces (fl.)	16.0
	U.S. gills	4.0
	U.S. quarts (liq.)	0.5
U.S. quarts (liq.)	British quarts	0.8326747
	cubic centimeters	946.35295
	cubic feet	0.03342
	cubic inches	57.75
	liters	0.9463264
	U.S. gallons (liq.)	0.25
	U.S. gills	8.0
	U.S. ounces (fl.)	32.0
	U.S. pints (liq.)	2.0
Yards	meters	0.9144

Capacity/Volume Conversion Tables
(Metric, U.S., Imperial Measurements)

The United Kingdom gallon is also called the British gallon, the British Imperial gallon, the Imperial gallon and, in Canada, the Canadian gallon.

To obtain the weight of U.S. gallons, multiply the specific gravity by 8.337.

To find the gallon (U.S.) capacity of a rectangular tank, multiply the length (in inches) by the width and the resulting figure by the depth. Divide this figure by 231 (1 gallon = 231 cubic inches).

To find the gallon (U.S.) capacity of a cylindrical tank, first measure the cubic inch content by multiplying the diameter (in inches) by itself (square the diameter) and multiply the resulting figure by 0.7854 and the one after that by the depth. This gives the cubic inch content which, divided by 231, gives the gallon capacity.

Gallons	U.S. Gallons to:		U.K. Gallons to:	
	Liters	U.K. Gal.	Liters	U.S. Gal.
1	3.7854	0.83270	4.5460	1.20092
2	7.5708	1.66539	9.0919	2.40183
3	11.3562	2.49809	13.6379	3.60275
4	15.1416	3.33079	18.1839	4.80367
5	18.9271	4.16348	22.7298	6.00458
6	22.7125	4.99618	27.2758	7.20550
7	26.4979	5.82888	31.8217	8.40642
8	30.2833	6.66158	36.3677	9.60734
9	34.0687	7.49427	40.9137	10.80825
10	37.8541	8.32697	45.4596	12.00917

Liters to U.S. and U.K. Gallons

Liters	U.S. gal	U.K. gal
1	0.26417	0.21998
2	0.52843	0.43995
3	0.79252	0.65993
4	1.05669	0.87990
5	1.32086	1.09988
6	1.58503	1.31985
7	1.84920	1.53983
8	2.11338	1.75980
9	2.37755	1.97978
10	2.64172	2.19975

Fluid Ounces to Centiliters— Centiliters to Fluid Ounces

cl	fl oz.	fl oz.	cl.
1	0.35196	1	2.8412
2	0.7039	2	5.6824
3	1.0559	3	8.5237
4	1.4078	4	11.3649
5	1.7598	5	14.2061
6	2.1118	6	17.0473
7	2.4637	7	19.8886
8	2.8157	8	22.7298
9	3.1676	9	25.5710
10	3.5196	10	28.4122

Conversion of Alcohol Percentages
(by Volume (V/V) to Weight (W/V))

V/V	W/V	V/V	W/V
1.0	0.79	5.5	4.38
1.1	0.87	5.6	4.46
1.2	0.95	5.7	4.54
1.3	1.03	5.8	4.62
1.4	1.11	5.9	4.70
1.5	1.19		
1.6	1.27	6.0	4.78
1.7	1.35	6.1	4.87
1.8	1.43	6.2	4.95
1.9	1.51	6.3	5.03
		6.4	5.11
2.0	1.59	6.5	5.19
2.1	1.67	6.6	5.27
2.2	1.75	6.7	5.35
2.3	1.82	6.8	5.43
2.4	1.90	6.9	5.51
2.5	1.98		
2.6	2.06	7.0	5.59
2.7	2.14	7.1	5.67
2.8	2.22	7.2	5.75
2.9	2.30	7.3	5.83
		7.4	5.91
3.0	2.38	7.5	5.99
3.1	2.46	7.6	6.07
3.2	2.54	7.7	6.15
3.3	2.62	7.8	6.24
3.4	2.70	7.9	6.32
3.5	2.78		
3.6	2.86	8.0	6.40
3.7	2.94	8.1	6.48
3.8	3.02	8.2	6.56
3.9	3.10	8.3	6.64
		8.4	6.72
4.0	3.18	8.5	6.80
4.1	3.26	8.6	6.88
4.2	3.34	8.7	6.96
4.3	3.42	8.8	7.04
4.4	3.50	8.9	7.12
4.5	3.58		
4.6	3.66	9.0	7.20
4.7	3.74	9.1	7.29
4.8	3.82	9.2	7.37
4.9	3.90	9.3	7.45
		9.4	7.53
5.0	3.98	9.5	7.61
5.1	4.06	9.6	7.69
5.2	4.14	9.7	7.77
5.3	4.22	9.8	7.85
5.4	4.30	9.9	7.93
		10.0	8.02

HOMEBREWER?

Join the thousands of American Homebrewers Association members who read **zymurgy** — the magazine for homebrewers and beer lovers.

Every issue of **zymurgy** is full of tips, techniques, new recipes, new products, equipment and ingredient reviews, beer news, technical articles — the whole world of homebrewing. PLUS, the AHA brings members the National Homebrewers Conference, the National Homebrew Competition, the Beer Judge Certification Program, the Homebrew Club Network, periodic discounts on books from Brewers Publications and much, much more.

Photocopy and mail this coupon today to join the AHA or call now for credit card orders, (303) 546-6514.

BOOKS for Brewers and Beer Lovers

Order Now ... Your Brew Will Thank You!

These books offered by Brewers Publications are some of the most sought after reference tools for homebrewers and professional brewers alike. Filled with tips, techniques, recipes and history, these books will help you expand your brewing horizons. Let the world's foremost brewers help you as you brew. So whatever your brewing level or interest, Brewers Publications has the information necessary for you to brew the best beer in the world — your beer.

- -

Please send me more free information on the following: (check all that apply)

◇ Merchandise & Book Catalog   ◇ Institute for Brewing Studies
◇ American Homebrewers Association   ◇ Great American Beer Festival℠

Ship to:

Name _____

Address _____

City _____ State/Province _____

Zip/Postal Code _____ Country _____

Daytime Phone (   ) _____

Please use the following in conjunction with order form when ordering books from Brewers Publications.

Payment Method

◇ Check or Money Order Enclosed (Payable to the Association of Brewers)
◇ Visa   ◇ MasterCard

Card Number _____ – _____ – _____ – _____   Expiration Date _____

Name on Card _____ Signature _____

Brewers Publications Inc., PO Box 1679, Boulder, CO 80306-1679, (303) 546-6514, FAX (303) 447-2825.
DICT94

BREWERS PUBLICATIONS ORDER FORM

PROFESSIONAL BREWING BOOKS

QTY.	TITLE	STOCK #	PRICE	EXT. PRICE
_____	Brewery Planner	500	80.00	_____
_____	North American Brewers Resource Directory	504	80.00	_____
_____	Principles of Brewing Science	463	29.95	_____

THE BREWERY OPERATIONS SERIES
from Micro and Pubbrewers Conferences

QTY.	TITLE	STOCK #	PRICE	EXT. PRICE
_____	Volume 4, 1987 Conference	534	25.95	_____
_____	Volume 6, 1989 Conference	536	25.95	_____
_____	Volume 7, 1990 Conference	537	25.95	_____
_____	Volume 8, 1991 Conference, Brewing Under Adversity	538	25.95	_____
_____	Volume 9, 1992 Conference, Quality Brewing — Share the Experience	539	25.95	_____

CLASSIC BEER STYLE SERIES

QTY.	TITLE	STOCK #	PRICE	EXT. PRICE
_____	Pale Ale	401	11.95	_____
_____	Continental Pilsener	402	11.95	_____
_____	Lambic	403	11.95	_____
_____	Vienna, Märzen, Oktoberfest	404	11.95	_____
_____	Porter	405	11.95	_____
_____	Belgian Ale	406	11.95	_____
_____	German Wheat Beer	407	11.95	_____
_____	Scotch Ale	408	11.95	_____
_____	Bock	409	11.95	_____

BEER AND BREWING SERIES, for homebrewers and beer enthusiasts,
from National Homebrewers Conferences

QTY.	TITLE	STOCK #	PRICE	EXT. PRICE
_____	Volume 8, 1988 Conference	448	21.95	_____
_____	Volume 10, 1990 Conference	450	21.95	_____
_____	Volume 11, 1991 Conference, Brew Free Or Die!	451	21.95	_____
_____	Volume 12, 1992 Conference, Just Brew It!	452	21.95	_____

GENERAL BEER AND BREWING INFORMATION

QTY.	TITLE	STOCK #	PRICE	EXT. PRICE
_____	Brewing Lager Beer	400	14.95	_____
_____	Brewing Mead	461	11.95	_____
_____	Dictionary of Beer and Brewing	462	19.95	_____
_____	Evaluating Beer	465	25.95	_____
_____	Great American Beer Cookbook	466	24.95	_____
_____	Victory Beer Recipes	467	11.95	_____
_____	Winners Circle	464	11.95	_____

SUBTOTAL _____

Call or write for a free *Beer Enthusiast* catalog today.
• U.S. funds only.
• All Brewers Publications books come with a money-back guarantee.
* **Postage & Handling:** $4 for the first book ordered, plus $1 for each book thereafter. Canadian and foreign orders please add $5 for the first book and $2 for each book thereafter. Orders cannot be shipped without appropriate P&H.

Colo. Residents Add 3% Sales Tax _____

P & H * _____

TOTAL _____

Brewers Publications Inc., PO Box 1510, Boulder, CO 80306-1510, (303) 546-6514, FAX (303) 447-2825.

DICT94